# Biblical
# womanhood

by Sarah Collins

**thegoodbook**
COMPANY

Biblical womanhood: a Good Book Guide
© The Good Book Company, 2004.
This 2nd edition © The Good Book Company 2010
Reprinted 2014, 2016

The Good Book Company
Tel (UK): 0333 123 0880
Tel: (US): 866 244 2165
Tel (int): + (44) 208 942 0880
Email: info@thegoodbook.co.uk

**Websites**
**UK:** www.thegoodbook.co.uk
**N America:** www.thegoodbook.com
**Australia:** www.thegoodbook.com.au
**New Zealand:** www.thegoodbook.co.nz

Unless otherwise indicated, all Scripture quotations are taken from The Holy Bible, New International Version®, Copyright © 1973, 1978, 1984, 2011 by Biblica, Inc.™ Used by permission. All rights reserved worldwide.

ISBN: 9781907377532

Cover design: André Parker
Printed in the Czech Republic

# CONTENTS

# Introduction: Good Book Guides

Every Bible-study group is different—yours may take place in a church building, in a home or in a cafe, on a train, over a leisurely mid-morning coffee or squashed into a 30-minute lunch break. Your group may include new Christians, mature Christians, non-Christians, mums and tots, students, businessmen or teens. That's why we've designed these *Good Book Guides* to be flexible for use in many different situations.

Our aim in each session is to uncover the meaning of a passage, and see how it fits into the "big picture" of the Bible. But that can never be the end. We also need to appropriately apply what we have discovered to our lives. Let's take a look at what is included:

⊕ **Talkabout:** Most groups need to "break the ice" at the beginning of a session, and here's the question that will do that. It's designed to get people talking around a subject that will be covered in the course of the Bible study.

⊕ **Investigate:** The Bible text for each session is broken up into manageable chunks, with questions that aim to help you understand what the passage is about. **The Leader's Guide** contains **guidance for questions**, and sometimes ⊗ additional "follow-up" questions.

⊡ **Explore more (optional):** These questions will help you connect what you have learned to other parts of the Bible, so you can begin to fit it all together like a jig-saw; or occasionally look at a part of the passage that's not dealt with in detail in the main study.

⊕ **Apply:** As you go through a Bible study, you'll keep coming across **apply** sections. These are questions to get the group discussing what the Bible teaching means in practice for you and your church. ⊡ **Getting personal** is an opportunity for you to think, plan and pray about the changes that you personally may need to make as a result of what you have learned.

⊕ **Pray:** We want to encourage prayer that is rooted in God's word—in line with His concerns, purposes and promises. So each session ends with an opportunity to review the truths and challenges highlighted by the Bible study, and turn them into prayers of request and thanksgiving.

The **Leader's Guide** and introduction provide historical background information, explanations of the Bible texts for each session, ideas for **optional extra** activities, and guidance on how best to help people uncover the truths of God's word.

# Why study
# biblical womanhood?

The goal of this *Biblical womanhood* course is to help Christian women to understand what the Bible says about being a woman. Since our own culture also has plenty to say about this subject, the course aims to help you identify the teaching of the world we live in and to defend, with confidence, the teaching of the Bible when the two stand in opposition. It is also designed to encourage women to rejoice in the truth as they apply it to their own lives and see that God's will is always for our best and His glory, whatever the world may say.

The course assumes an acceptance of the Bible's authority in all areas of life and doctrine. Some of the material is undoubtedly controversial, going against the grain of our western culture, and even against the grain of commonly accepted teaching within the church. However, this course does not set out to be politically correct but to be faithful to Scripture.

That said, questioning, debate and disagreement is not necessarily something to be avoided, although it must be rooted in, and weighed by, what is clear in God's word. The course will not answer every question for every person, and in fact, it is quite likely to raise more questions than it answers! Our natural tendency can be to want everything "sewn up" and to have a neat list of answers on how precisely to interpret and apply the Bible. We need to work hard at keeping grey areas grey (when we so often wish they were black and white), while also letting what is black and white in the Bible remain black and white in our own thinking and living.

I hope you find the following pages helpful in living for the Lord Jesus Christ as women after His own heart.

# 1
## Genesis 1 and 2
# FOUNDATIONS

## ⊕ talkabout

1. What makes men and women fundamentally the same as each other? List some of the similarities you've noticed.

2. Think of some of the ways men and women are different. Do you think we are born with these differences, or do we learn them from the world around us?

## ⊕ investigate: the Maker's design

### ▶ Read Genesis 1 v 24-31

Genesis 1 v 24-31 tells us what God made on the sixth day, including land animals and humankind. Genesis 2 gives us more detail on how the first man and woman were created.

3. What job description did God give to the first humans (v 28-31)? Is there any difference between men and women here?

**4.** In what ways are humans different from the rest of creation (v 24-27)?

**5.** What does it mean that we are "created in God's image"? Remember to look at the surrounding verses to help you find an answer.

⊡ **apply**

**6.** How does Genesis 1 challenge people and cultures who view and treat women as second-class citizens?

• What does it say to those who view men as "surplus to requirements"?

⊡ **getting personal**

The only right response to Genesis 1 is to praise, glorify and give thanks to our Creator God. Will you thank Him for designing men and woman together to reflect His likeness? Will you thank Him for making you a woman?

# ⊍ investigate

> ❯ **Read Genesis 2 v 4-7 and 15-25**

**7.** What did the man (Adam) spend his time doing before Eve came along? How did he relate to the rest of creation?

Verse 18 comes as a bit of a shock: in a perfect creation, God sees something that is not good. Adam is incomplete. He needs a "helper" suitable to assist him in ruling God's creation.

**8.** Why do you think God parades the animals in front of Adam in search of a helper?

• How does Adam's response in v 23 show Eve is the perfect match?

Eve alone can complement Adam. We might think of "helper" as a derogatory term (like "Santa's little helper") but it is far from that! The word is used to describe God Himself in Exodus 18 v 4 and Psalm 33 v 20, where it carries overtones of military strength. Eve is not "just a cleaner", therefore, but a wingman (or wingwoman!) fighting the battle alongside Adam.

**9.** In what ways is Eve shown to be different from Adam, in how, when and why she was created? What do you think is the significance of this?

**10.** What significance is there in the fact that Adam names her (2 v 23 and 3 v 20)?

**11.** Summarise what you have learned about the complementary relationship between Adam and Eve. How do verses 24 and 25 show that God's design was good?

optional

## ⊡ explore more

**❯ Read 1 Corinthians 11 v 3, 8-9 and 11-12**

Here Paul is using Genesis 2 to teach the church that the differences between men and women are vital to the life of the church.

*How does Paul help us to understand that men and women are created equal? And that they are created different?*

*How does Paul describe the relationship between Christ and God (v 3)?*

*How does this help us to understand rightly equality and difference in male-female relationships?*

*If you are unsure about whether you truly know God, what have you learned in this session that can help you?*

The lines of responsibility God created can be summarised like this:

GOD
⊡
Man
Woman
⊡
The rest of creation

## ➡ apply

**12.** How does the complementary design for men and women outlined in Genesis 2 fit your observations in questions 1 and 2?

**13.** God designed women to be different from men. How does that affect the way we see ourselves? How does it encourage and challenge us?

- How does it affect the way we see the men we know? How can we encourage them to be responsible and take a godly lead?

## ☺ getting personal

What can you do to live more in line with God's good design for men and women? Write down one change that you could make this week, and pray daily for God's help with that.

# ⊤ pray

**Praise God...**

for His fantastic creation, and His wonderful design for men and women.

**Seek forgiveness...**

for times when you have resented God's good design and have rebelled against His purposes in you, both as a human and a woman.

**Ask God...**

to help you grow as a godly woman, especially in the way you relate to men.

**2** Genesis 3 v 1-24
# WOMEN AND THE FALL

## ⊕ talkabout

1. Compare the world we live in with the picture of the first man and woman living in perfect harmony in Genesis 2. How do they match up?

## ⊕ investigate: the image marred

### ❯ Read Genesis 3 v 1-24

This event is known as the fall because it marks when the human race fell from their high position in special relationship with God, taking all creation crashing down with them.

2. What tactics did the snake (ie: Satan) use to tempt Eve?

• How does he use them still today to tempt people?

3. Where does Eve go wrong?

- How do her actions here fall short of the role she is given in Genesis 2 v 18?

**4.** Where does Adam go wrong? (Clue: Where was he while Eve was being tempted, v 6?)

In these verses we see humankind wanting to be gods in charge of their own destiny. But their attempt to up-end God's order for leadership has actually put the serpent in top spot:

Creature
⬇
Woman
Man
⬇
God

## ⊡ getting personal

In what area at the moment are you finding it difficult to trust that God's way is best? Will you pray about that issue each day this week, asking God to help you see through Satan's lies?

**5.** Read verse 17. How does God hold Adam responsible for the rebellion?

• Why did he make Adam responsible?

6.  How did the fall affect Adam and Eve's relationship with God (v 8-13, 22-24)?

7.  How did it affect their relationship with each other (v 7, 12, 16)?

8.  How do the curses (v 16-19) reflect the different roles originally given to Adam and Eve? In what way have those roles been spoiled by the fall?

The word "desire" in verse 16 means desire for power. Eve's sin in taking Adam's leadership role has now become her punishment! The woman will now resist her role and strive for power over the man. On the other hand, the man will now twist his role of loving leader into harsh ruler.

Whether the roles are confused or abused, the battle of the sexes will echo through every age and every society.

## ⊡ explore more: the image restored

❯ **Read Colossians 3 v 5-17**

*What has happened to us if we are Christians (v 10)? What does this mean for the curses of Genesis 3?*

*As new people, Paul says, we are "being renewed in knowledge in the image of [our] Creator" (v 10). But how does this actually happen in reality? Have a look at v 15-17 and notice three ways.*

## ⊖ apply

**9.** Think about the battle of the sexes today. How is the equality of the sexes under attack?

• How is the difference and complementarity of the sexes under attack?

We've seen that one effect of the fall on women is that we seek to resist our God-given role and to strive for power over men. That leads to conflict within marriage and a battle of the sexes throughout the whole of society, where both men and women show unhelpful attitudes towards each other.

**10.** In what ways might we display this "Genesis 3" way of relating to men? (You might like to think about marriage and/or the workplace.)

# getting personal

If you are a Christian, praise God that you are being restored to His creation design, outlined in Genesis 1 and 2. What changes in your life can you already see and thank God for?

# ⬆ pray

**For yourself**

Use Colossians 3 v 10 as the basis for your prayers, giving thanks and making requests.

**For each other**

Base your prayers on Colossians 3 v 16.

# 3 Matthew 19; Ephesians 5; Proverbs 31
# WOMEN AND MARRIAGE

## talkabout

**1.** In some western countries, only half of all marriages survive. What makes marriage so hard? How can you trace this back to Genesis 3?

## investigate: what is marriage?

**Read Matthew 19 v 4-6**

**2.** List five things from these verses that make up a marriage.

- v 4
- v 5
- v 5
- v 6
- v 6

- How does this compare to our culture's view of what makes a marriage?

**3.** Re-read Genesis 1 v 26-28 and 2 v 18. What is marriage for? Compare this to our culture's view.

# ⬇ investigate: the Christ-centred marriage

### ❯ Read Ephesians 5 v 21-33

When God created men and women and gave them marriage, He did it as a visual aid pointing to Christ and His church. Submission is not just agreeing to everything! For the church, submitting to Christ is actively and willingly to seek His interests and follow His lead.

**4.** What does it mean for a wife to submit (v 22-24, 33)?

- We've seen that an aspect of being a "helper" is actively to enable and encourage a husband's leadership. How does this tie in with that?

**5.** What should a husband's love look like (v 25-30)? Why?

**6.** How does v 32 motivate a husband and wife to work hard at their roles in marriage?

→ **apply**

**7.** How could this passage be used to help a Christian marriage that is struggling?

**8.** How could this passage help shape what a single person might look for in a husband, or what they might seek to be as a wife?

⊡ **getting personal**

If you are married, how are you doing with submission to your husband? Are there any areas in your relationship where things need to change?

If you are single, how are you doing with helping friends submit to their husbands, and are you prepared to submit to any future husband? Is there anything that needs to change in how you think or what you say?

⊡ **explore more: what about mixed marriage?**

❯ **Read 1 Peter 3 v 1-7**

Christian women are commanded not to marry unbelievers (1 Corinthians 7 v 39), but for various reasons some women find themselves in this situation. It can be tempting to think that the idea of submitting doesn't apply to a wife with a non-Christian husband.

*How does Peter advise these women in v 1-2? What encouragement does he offer?*

# ⬇ investigate: a wife of noble character

## ❯ Read Proverbs 31 v 10-31

**DICTIONARY**

**Flax (v 13):** a plant that was used to make linen.
**Distaff, spindle (v 19):** tools used for spinning flax or wool fibres into thread.

**9.** What are this woman's roles and responsibilities, both inside and outside the home?

• How is she fulfilling the role of "helper" to her husband here?

**10.** What kinds of attitudes and priorities do you think give her a "noble" character in God's eyes?

• Why is she worth "far more than rubies" to her husband?

Is the wife of noble character the ultimate multi-tasking woman, with a husband who just sits around all day? No, her husband "sits" at the city gate (ie: he is a respected community leader); and the fact that we are told this here implies that he is where he is because of her. She is a true "helper" to him. She enables him to be the man he is as she diligently and joyfully runs his home, cares for his children, serves the community and, above all, puts God first.

# ➔ apply

**11.** What can we learn from the woman of Proverbs 31 today...

• for living out the helper design within marriage?

• for all women, married or single, who want to be women of noble character?

## ⌐ getting personal

Write down one thing that you have learned from Proverbs 31 that you know is missing from your life at the moment. What steps can you take to address this?

## ⬆ pray

**Thank God...**

for your ultimate Husband—Jesus Christ. In whatever your situation now, married or single, ask God to make you a blessing as a true helper and woman of "noble character".

**Married women**

Thank God for your husband. Ask God to help you be a true helper and a blessing to him.

**Single women**

Ask God to make you someone who helps other women (and perhaps yourself one day) to be a true helper to their husband.

# 4 1 Corinthians 7 v 1-9, 25-40
# WOMEN AND SINGLENESS

## ⊕ talkabout

1. How does our society view singleness? Include both positive and negative images.

   • What kinds of views do Christians have on singleness?

## ⬇ investigate: "on the shelf" or free to serve?

▶ **Read 1 Corinthians 7 v 1-9, 25-40**

2. This world could end at any time (v 29-31). How should that affect the way we see our lives, single or married? How does it affect our approach to time, priorities, money and ambitions?

**DICTIONARY**

**Sexual immorality (v 2):** sexual sin.
**A concession (v 6):** something which is permitted.

**3.** Verse 7 tells us that both marriage and singleness are gifts from God. How should this change the way you see your situation?

**4.** Compare our romantic ideals with what Paul says about marriage (v 28). What kinds of troubles do you think he has in mind?

**5.** How do Paul's views on singleness (v 32-35) differ from the way we often think about it?

**6.** What does it mean for a single person to be "devoted to the Lord in both body and spirit" (v 34)? Why does being unmarried make a difference (v 32)?

## ⊖ apply

**7.** List the things that single people can enjoy and ways they can serve, which they couldn't do if they were married.

• How can you and your church best support and encourage single people?

## ⊡ getting personal

Singleness, like marriage, is a gift of God. Whether you are single or married, how will you allow this truth to affect the way you relate to (other) single Christians?

## ⊡ explore more

*In the last session we learned that marriage is a picture of Christ and His bride, the church. Look up the following passages. How do they help us to understand this eternal perspective on marriage and singleness?*

• *Ephesians 5 v 25-31*

• *Mark 12 v 25*

• *Isaiah 54 v 4-8*

• *Revelation 21 v 1-4*

**8.** Jesus Christ is the ultimate Husband of all believers (See Explore More above). Write down three things that can encourage you in your relationship with Him—both now and in the future.

## ⊡ getting personal

If you're a single woman, are you willing to embrace cheerfully and peacefully the freedom of your singleness to live a life devoted to your Lord?

If you're married, are you willing to accept cheerfully and peacefully the "troubles" of marriage to bring glory and honour to your ultimate Husband?

## ⊕ pray

**Thank God...**

for the gift that you have been given, whether it is marriage or singleness. Thank Him for Jesus, the most loving of all men, and thank Him that He has given you a relationship with Him.

**Ask God...**

to help single Christians you know as they seek to live devotedly for the Lord in a culture which does not understand them, and which imposes many pressures and temptations on them.

# 5 1 Peter 3; 1 Timothy 2
# WOMEN AND BEAUTY

## ⊕ talkabout

1. Women today are under enormous pressure to look beautiful. How does this pressure affect our society?

• What are the effects in your own life?

The Bible celebrates outward beauty. God created a world that was "pleasing to the eye" so we could enjoy it with Him. Physical beauty is praised in describing Esther, for example, or Job's daughters, and Song of Songs is full of it! Like all God's good gifts it is to be enjoyed with gratitude (1 Timothy 4 v 4). Like all good gifts, though, we can make it an idol that steals our trust and demands our worship.

## ⊕ investigate: unfading beauty

### ❯ Read 1 Peter 3 v 1-7

2. What should not be the source of our beauty (v 3)? Why not?

DICTIONARY

**Submit to (v 1):** follow the lead of.

**3.** Where should our beauty come from? How is it connected to our relationship with God (v 2-5)?

**4.** "A gentle and quiet" spirit (v 4) is a description more of character than of personality. Describe what such a character would look like. (See also Matthew 11 v 29 for "gentle" and Zephaniah 3 v 17 (ESV) for "quiet".)

• What would the opposite look like?

→ **apply**

**5.** What will help us to cultivate the true beauty of "a gentle and quiet spirit"?

⊡ **getting personal**

Regardless of your personality, would someone who knows you well agree that you have a "gentle and quiet spirit"? In what situations do you need to show more clearly your trust and hope in God?

## ⬇ investigate: modesty, decency, propriety

### ❯ Read 1 Timothy 2 v 9-10

In this letter, Paul writes to Timothy about "how people ought to conduct themselves in God's household" (3 v 15). He seems to focus especially on how the church should behave when gathered together, as well as in their daily lives.

**6.** What does it mean to dress with modesty, decency and propriety (which means appropriateness)? What does our culture think of such qualities?

**7.** Why do you think Paul calls Christian women to be like this?

• What will it mean for us in practice?

**8.** Why is it inappropriate for "women who profess to worship God" to let our appearance devour our time, thoughts and money?

• What makes good deeds (v 10) a woman's best accessory?

⊡ **explore more** | optional

❯ **Read Hebrews 10 v 19-25**

*What things are mentioned in these verses that will help us to beautify our lives with good deeds?*

• *v 19-23*

• *v 24-25*

⊡ **apply**

**9.** How do we need to re-shape our understanding of what beauty is?

**10.** How can we pursue true, unfading beauty for ourselves, and encourage others in that pursuit too?

**11.** How can we appreciate external appearance without making an idol of it?

**getting personal**

What are the particular areas where you are tempted to make an idol of physical appearance?

Is there one thing that you can do, or stop doing, this week which will help you resist this temptation?

What one thing could you do to help others understand what true beauty is? Is there any particular friend of yours you need to gently help with this?

⬆ **pray**

**Praise God...**

for His wonderful creation of you—and His wonderful re-creation of you in Christ.

**Seek forgiveness...**

for times when you have made an idol out of outward beauty.

**Ask God...**

to help you to resist the world's ideas about beauty, and to grow in you the true beauty of good deeds and a quiet and gentle spirit.

# 6 Galatians 3 – 4; 1 Timothy 2
# WOMEN AND THE FAMILY OF GOD

## ⊕ talkabout

1. List at least ten of the key men and women of God you can think of from the Bible. What kinds of roles did they have? Did the roles differ at all between men and women?

## ⊕ investigate: equal in Christ

> **▶ Read Galatians 3 v 26 – 4 v 7**

2. What is at the heart of the equality described in 3 v 26-29 and 4 v 6-7?

**DICTIONARY**

**Gentile (v 28):** non-Jews.
**Abraham's seed (v 29):** descendants of Abraham, the Old Testament figure (see Genesis 11 – 25).
**Elemental spiritual forces (4 v 3):** a belief system that says we must save ourselves, by worshipping fake gods or by trying to keep religious rules.

• Why would this teaching have been so shocking in that culture?

**3.** These verses are often used to argue for equal ministry opportunities for men and women in the church. Do you think this can be argued from the passage? Why, or why not?

## ⊡ apply

**4.** Think of women who struggle with feelings of insecurity because of their sex—perhaps someone from another culture, a professional who has hit a "glass ceiling" at work, or a stay-at-home mum.

How could you use this teaching to help them and introduce them to the gospel?

## ⊡ investigate: headship through the Bible

Throughout the Bible there is a pattern of male leaders in God's family, even when the neighbouring nations have priestesses, queens and even goddesses. Jesus Himself constantly defied social expectations, not least in His dignified treatment of women, and the way He encouraged them to learn about God. Nevertheless, He chose twelve male apostles to lead His church.

**❯ Read 1 Timothy 2 v 8-15**

**5.** What attitude are women to have when they meet together with the church family (v 11-12)?

**6.** What two reasons are given in verses 13-14? Why do you think Paul goes right back to Genesis?

Verse 15 can seem quite tricky to understand at first! Judging by the previous verse, Paul seems to be saying that the woman will be saved from the original deception that led to Eve taking the fruit. Eve was deceived into thinking it was her place to lead Adam into the decision to mistrust and disobey God. To avoid this distortion of God's design, women need to "be women". "Childbearing" could be taken as shorthand for fulfilling God's design for women (even without children), instead of trying to be men.

## ⊖ apply

**7.** What will it mean for us to be "women" in the church rather than "men"? What kind of women does v 15 say we should be?

## ⊡ explore more: so what can women do in the church?

*optional*

*Look up the following passages and write down all the different ways women serve God in the Bible.*

- *Exodus 15 v 19-21*

- *Proverbs 31 v 10-31*

- *John 4 v 39-42*

- *Acts 1 v 14*

- *Acts 16 v 14-15*

- *Acts 18 v 24-26*
- *Romans 16 v 1-16*
- *1 Timothy 5 v 9-10*
- *2 Timothy 1 v 5 and 3 v 14-15*
- *Titus 2 v 3-5*

Although the Bible is clear that the overall teaching and leading of God's family is to be by men, there is a big "grey area" beyond that. People differ on whether, for example, women should preach, teach mixed Bible study or youth groups, and so on. We need to use our consciences to form our own biblical opinions, without judging others who are trying to do the same.

**8.** How can women serve in your church? How does this complement the way the men serve?

**9.** How would you go about forming opinions in the "grey area"? (Romans 14 will help to give you guiding principles in this.)

**10.** How can you develop an attitude of support and willing submission towards church leaders and teachers?

**getting personal**

If Paul were to write to your church, would he include you in a list of hard-working women to be praised for your help in the Lord?

How much do you think your church leaders feel helped in their responsibilities by your involvement?

Does anything need to change?

⊕ **pray**

Base your prayers of praise and thanksgiving to God on Galatians 3 v 26-29.

Use 1 Timothy 2 v 15 as the basis for your prayers of request, and ask God to help you to avoid following Eve's example.

**7** **Titus 2 v 1-5**

# WOMEN AND THEIR SISTERS

## ⊕ talkabout

1. Think about your friendships with men and women. How do they differ? What do you value about friendship with other women?

2. Think about an older Christian woman who has influenced you. How did her friendship or example help you?

## ⊕ investigate: woman to woman

### ▶ Read Titus 2 v 1-5

The only group Titus isn't told to teach directly is the younger women. This is the job of older women, presumably because they could do a better job of living out what it means to be a godly woman than he could!

3. What qualities should an older woman be taught to cultivate (v 3)? What should be her attitude towards God, others and herself?

**4.** What areas are highlighted as the focus for the older women in training younger women? Why are these highlighted, do you think?

• How do you think this kind of training can best take place?

**5.** What will be the result of this kind of training?

The training of younger women in v 4-5 centres on the home. The married woman's relationship with her husband starts and ends her list of responsibilities because it is the key to family life. This does not rule out career or leisure pursuits outside the home, but her role as wife and mother comes first. Nor does this rule out single women in both training and being trained: godliness needs to be taught and modelled in whatever context a woman finds herself.

### ⊡ getting personal

How important are your home and family responsibilities to you? Are they your primary responsibility, or something to fit round career, study and leisure?

Do your attitude and example encourage your Christian friends and/or daughters to prioritise home and family responsibilities?

## ⊡ explore more

*Look back to Proverbs 31 v 10-31. How does the wife of noble character flesh out Titus 2 v 3-5?*

*How do you imagine her being an "older woman", involved in the training of younger women? What would they have learned from her?*

## ➔ apply

**6.** In what kinds of contexts can such woman-to-woman training go on? What are the opportunities for this in your church family?

**7.** Who are you an "older woman" to? How can you encourage this younger woman, by your example and words, to live a godly life?

• Who are you a "younger woman" to? How can you learn from this older woman's words and example to you?

## ⊡ explore more: Christ-centred friendship

*Friendship is a great gift from God, and for believers it can be greatly used to "spur one another on towards love and good deeds" (Hebrews 10 v 24). But sometimes our friendships can be used to pull each other back from living for God. Pick out some ways in which friendships can have a negative effect.*

*Look at the following proverbs. What kind of qualities is God looking for in friendships between believers?*

- *Proverbs 12 v 18*

- *Proverbs 13 v 20*

- *Proverbs 17 v 17*

- *Proverbs 27 v 5-6*

- *Proverbs 27 v 9*

- *Proverbs 27 v 17*

**8.** How can you develop your friendships with other women to include the qualities discussed in Explore More above? Think practically and write down three suggestions.

## ⊞ getting personal

How much do you think about what kind of a friend you are to other Christian women? Do things just happen at a social level, or do you and your friends make it your aim to encourage growing wisdom and godliness in each other?

## ⊤ pray

**Together**

Thank God for one another and pray that as sisters in Christ you would help each other to grow in the Lord.

**Alone**

Pray for a friendship with a more mature Christian woman you can learn from, and a younger woman you can teach, train and pray for.

# 8 WOMEN AND THEIR BROTHERS

## ⊕ talkabout

**1.** How does the world around us encourage us to relate to men?

## ⊕ investigate: sexual purity

Sex is celebrated in the Bible—it was God's idea and His gift! The Song of Songs is full of unashamed delight in it and Paul commands married couples not to withhold it from one another (1 Corinthians 7 v 3-5). In Genesis 2 v 24 it expresses the "one flesh" union of man and woman in marriage. It is too precious for any context other than the exclusive, permanent and public agreement of marriage.

**❯ Read Ephesians 5 v 1-14**

**2.** What kinds of things should characterise the people of God? Why?

**DICTIONARY**

**Obscenity (v 4):** disgusting and offensive words.
**Idolater (v 5):** a person who worships something other than God.
**Wrath (v 6):** God's just, righteous anger.

• What kinds of things are "out of place" for the people of God? Why?

## → apply

3. "But among you there must not be even a hint of sexual immorality" (Ephesians 5 v 3). List the implications for...

• what we watch/read/talk about.

• how we dress.

• how we communicate with men.

## ⊡ getting personal

Spend an honest moment thinking about your behaviour in the last week. Has there been even a hint of sexual immorality? If yes, think about what changes you must make immediately. Make this a priority in your prayers.

## ⊡ investigate: the unforgivable sin?

### ❯ Read 1 Corinthians 6 v 9-11, 18-20

Sexual sin can cause deep emotional, psychological and physical damage (1 Corinthians 6 v 18). However, it is never singled out as the worst of sins. Jesus related to a number of women whose lives had been scarred in one way or another by sexual immorality, and He always offered complete forgiveness and cleansing.

DICTIONARY

**Sanctified (v 11):** made holy.
**Justified (v 11):** declared to be "not guilty" in God's sight.

**4.** What kinds of people were in the Corinthian church (verses 9-11)? What does this show about the gospel?

**5.** How did they qualify for the kingdom of God (v 11)? How does this both encourage and humble us?

**6.** Look at verses 11 and 19-20. How do they motivate us to live changed lives?

🙂 **getting personal**

Do you feel guilty for the way in which you lived in the past? Do you feel damaged or unclean because of past experiences? If you are a Christian, you are washed, sanctified and justified. Now start to enjoy living in the light of that reality!

**7.** Think of as many reasons as you can for why Christians "go out" with someone. Which of these reasons do you think are wise, and which unwise?

The idea of dating or "going out" did not exist when the Bible was written, so it is tempting to think it has nothing to say on the subject. In fact, the Bible is very clear on how unmarried men and women are to relate to each other; as brothers and sisters, with "absolute purity" (1 Timothy 5 v 2).

**⏵ Read 1 Thessalonians 4 v 1-10**

**DICTIONARY**

**Pagans (v 5):** non-believers.

**8.** From this passage, what should be the priorities for Christians who "go out"?

**9.** Why does living in the world make it difficult to keep these priorities (eg: v 5)?

**10.** How do you think that relating to one another as brother and sister transforms "going out" relationships (v 6, 9, 10)?

## ⮕ apply

**11.** What do you think it looks like in practice to "avoid sexual immorality" in a relationship (v 3-4)?

12. You're advising a friend about being godly in a relationship with a man. How would you use 1 Thessalonians 4, and the other passages we have looked at, to advise them?

⬆ **pray**

### Re-read 1 Corinthians 6 v 11

Pray for Christian brothers and sisters struggling with the guilt and damage caused by sexual sin.

Give thanks for the gospel, which brings us cleansing and forgiveness.

### Re-read 1 Thessalonians 4 v 7

Ask God to help you to live a life of absolute purity for the glory of His name.

## 9 Titus 2; Ephesians 6
# WOMEN AND THEIR CHILDREN

⊕ **talkabout**

**1.** List some of the positive and negative ways in which our culture views motherhood.

- How do you think these views influence the decisions women make about having children?

Our God-created biological differences from men show that bearing children is a significant aspect of being a woman—one of the ways in which woman is a "helper" to man, fulfilling God's command to "fill the earth" (Genesis 1 and 2).

In God's eyes, motherhood is essential and wonderful. But it is also very much affected by the fall. Women now know pain in childbearing (Genesis 3 v 16), which probably includes the whole process of raising children—the physical exhaustion and emotional roller coaster of parenthood as well as the pain of giving birth.

But in Christ, as with all aspects of our humanity, motherhood can be redeemed (bought back) and become, despite the hardship and pain, beautifully and powerfully used in God's purposes.

# ⊕ investigate: home and work

### ❯ Read Titus 2 v 3-5 (and 1 Timothy 5 v 9-10, 14, if you have time)

**2.** Western society often urges women to get to the top of the career ladder and correct the so-called "imbalance" between sexes in the workplace. How do Paul's words sound to our 21st-century ears?

**3.** What kind of character is needed for fulfilling the role of wife, mother and homemaker so that all can see how attractive it is to live God's way?

## ⊡ explore more

optional

### ❯ Read Proverbs 31 v 10-31

We revisit the wife of noble character to see what redeemed motherhood looks like. Although this side of the fall it is very hard work, if carried out in God's strength it can be deeply satisfying, effective and beautiful.

*Describe how this wife seeks to fulfil her role as a mother.*

*What kinds of things might her children learn from her?*

*What do you think it would be like to live in her home?*

*How do you think her relationship with the Lord underpins all she does?*

## ⮕ apply

**4.** Mothers who don't have employment outside the home sometimes describe themselves as "only a mum". How can understanding God's view of the role of motherhood help them?

**5.** Some mothers need to work full-time outside the home just to make ends meet; but where a mum has a choice, what principles and priorities should guide her decision?

**6.** For those who are not biological mothers, where can we find opportunities to cultivate our God-given capacity for nurturing? The following passages give some guidance on this:

• Galatians 6 v 10

• 1 Timothy 5 v 10

• 1 Thessalonians 2 v 6b-12

## ⊡ investigate: biblical parenting

❯ **Read Ephesians 6 v 1-4**

**7.** What do these verses set out as the primary responsibility of parents?

- How is this done?

- What is the goal?

**8.** Read the following Bible passages and note down anything they tell us about how or why parents are to teach their children about the Lord.

| How we teach our children | Why we teach our children |
|---|---|
| Deuteronomy 6 v 4-9 | Proverbs 6 v 20-22 |
| Deuteronomy 6 v 20-21 | Proverbs 14 v 26 |
| Psalm 145 v 4-7 | 2 Timothy 1 v 5; 3 v 15 |

9. How do all these verses show the parents' own relationship with God to be crucial in this task?

## ⤷ apply

10. List some practical ideas for teaching children the Bible day to day. What kind of formal or informal, regular or unplanned opportunities can be taken?

**11.** It is not only biological mothers who can be involved in the spiritual nurture of children. Timothy's grandmother, Lois, was instrumental in teaching him the scriptures "from infancy" (2 Timothy 1 v 5, 3 v 5). List some of the different ways in which Christian women might help in nurturing the children of others in Christ.

## ⊡ getting personal

What opportunities do you have at the moment for helping children to understand more of Jesus and live for Him? How can you make the most of these opportunities?

Are you showing by your life, priorities, attitudes and ambitions that He is worth following?

## ⬆ pray

Read **Psalm 145 v 4-7** again.

**Give thanks...**

for the children you know, whether your own, those of your family or friends, or children within your church family.

**Pray...**

for specific children you know and for opportunities to nurture them and point them to Jesus.

# 10 Various; Luke 10 v 38-42
# WOMEN AND THEIR LORD

## ⊕ talkabout

1. What are some of the things that threaten the priority of spending time with Jesus, in His word and prayer?

- What effect does it have on your life when time with God is squeezed out?

## ⬇ investigate: women who knew Jesus

> **Read Luke 7 v 11-17, 36-50; 8 v 43-48; John 4 v 1-26, 39**

In the culture Jesus lived in, women were second-class citizens. It is remarkable that women feature so strongly in the Gospels (and indeed the rest of the Bible!). Even more remarkable is the way in which Jesus treats them. From the following passages we can glean insights into how Jesus relates to different women with all their various needs.

### DICTIONARY

**Bier (Luke 7 v 14):** frame used to carry a corpse.
**Prophet (7 v 16):** a person chosen to give a direct message from God.
**Alabaster (7 v 37):** white stone which can be carved into ornaments.
**Pharisees (7 v 36, Jn 4 v 1):** Jewish religious leaders; very strict on obeying God's law and many other man-made laws.
**Samaritan (Jn 4 v 7):** a person from Samaria; hated by the Jews at this time.

2.  Look up the passages in the table below and note down the kind of woman Jesus is with, how He relates to her and how she relates to Him.

| Verses | What kind of woman | How Jesus relates to her | How she relates to Jesus |
|--------|--------------------|--------------------------|--------------------------|
| Luke 7 v 11-17 | | | |
| Luke 7 v 36-50 | | | |
| Luke 8 v 43-48 | | | |
| John 4 v 1-26, 39 | | | |

3.  Given that women did not have much social standing at this time, what strikes you about the women Jesus spoke to?

# ⊟ apply

**4.** Discuss what you've learned about the way Jesus relates to these women, and how they relate to Him. How does this encourage us as women who are known and loved by Jesus?

## ⊡ getting personal

There is nothing about us Jesus doesn't know, and there's nothing about us He can't forgive. Do you know yet what it is to be freed by His love and grace from insecurity, fear, sinful habits and being self-absorbed?

## ⊌ investigate: "one thing needed"

> **Read Luke 10 v 38-42**

**5.** Think about Martha: what had distracted her (v 40)? How did this colour what she thought about Mary and about Jesus?

**6.** How did Jesus respond (v 41)? What strikes you about His manner?

**7.** What was Mary doing (v 39)? What was her attitude towards Jesus?

**8.** What "better thing" had she chosen that Martha hadn't? Why would it "not be taken away from her" (v 42)?

Although it may be tempting to sympathise with Martha, Jesus gently yet firmly rebukes her. She was thinking more of what she could do for Him than what He could do for her. It is ironic that she was distracted from Him by what she was doing for Him. How true that can be of us! Being like Mary does not necessarily mean we sit around praying and reading our Bibles all day. Rather, it means that we daily choose to make time to sit at His feet, listening to Him through the Bible and talking with Him in prayer. As with Mary, the lasting value of doing this will never be wasted (v 42).

⊡ **apply**

**9.** What kinds of things distract us from Jesus and the "one thing needed"? How can we be like Martha in our attitude?

**10.** Think of all the priorities in your week (things which you always make sure happen). List four ways of also making sure that your time with Jesus happens.

**11.** How can we make sure we do spend time with him (think practically)?

**12.** How does the lasting value of this (v 42) encourage us to persevere in growing in our relationship with Jesus?

## ⊡ getting personal

Do you find yourself "worried and upset about many things"? Are you spending little or no time with Jesus—and why is that?

In what practical ways can you begin to choose "what is better" in the coming week?

## ⊕ pray

**Thank God...**

for His Son—your Saviour, Lord and ultimate Husband.

**Pray...**

for each other as you reach the end of this series of Bible studies. Ask God to help each of you grow in your hearts and lives in faith, love and joyful obedience to Christ.

# Biblical womanhood: Leader's Guide

## INTRODUCTION

Leading a Bible study can be a bit like herding cats—everyone has a different idea of what the passage could be about, and a different line of enquiry that they want to pursue. But a good group leader is more than someone who just referees this kind of discussion. You will want to:

- correctly understand and handle the Bible passage. But also...

- encourage and train the people in your group to do this for themselves. Don't fall into the trap of spoon-feeding people by simply passing on the information in the Leader's Guide. Then...

- make sure that no Bible study is finished without everyone knowing how the passage is relevant for them. What changes do you all need to make in the light of the things you have been learning? And finally...

- encourage the group to turn all that has been learned and discussed into prayer.

Your Bible-study group is unique, and you are likely to know better than anyone the capabilities, backgrounds and circumstances of the people you are leading. That's why we've designed these guides with a number of optional features. If they're a quiet bunch, you might want to spend longer on talkabout. If your time is limited, you can choose to skip explore more, or get people to look at these questions at home. Can't get enough of Bible study? Well, some studies have optional extra homework projects. As leader, you can adapt and select the material to the needs of your particular group.

So what's in the Leader's Guide? The main thing that this Leader's Guide will help you to do is to understand the major teaching points in the passage you are studying, and how to apply them. As well as guidance on the questions, the Leader's Guide for each session contains the following important sections:

## THE BIG IDEA

One key sentence will give you the main point of the session. This is what you should be aiming to have fixed in people's minds as they leave the Bible study. And it's the point you need to head back towards when the discussion goes off at a tangent.

## SUMMARY

An overview of the passage, including plenty of useful historical background information.

## OPTIONAL EXTRA

Usually this is an introductory activity that ties in with the main theme of the Bible study, and is designed to "break the ice" at the beginning of a session. Or it may be a "homework project" that people can tackle during the week.

So let's take a look at the various different features of a Good Book Guide:

## ⊕ talkabout

Each session kicks off with a discussion question, based on the group's opinions or experiences. It's designed to get people talking and thinking in a general way about the main subject of the Bible study.

# ⊻ investigate

The first thing you and your group need to know is what the Bible passage is about, which is the purpose of these questions. But watch out—people may come up with answers based on their experiences or teaching they have heard in the past, without referring to the passage at all. It's amazing how often we can get through a Bible study without actually looking at the Bible! If you're stuck for an answer, the Leader's Guide contains guidance on questions. These are the answers to direct your group to. This information isn't meant to be read out to people—ideally, you want them to discover these answers from the Bible for themselves. Sometimes there are optional follow-up questions (see ☑ in guidance for questions) to help you help your group get to the answer.

# ⊡ explore more

These questions generally point people to other relevant parts of the Bible. They are useful for helping your group to see how the passage fits into the "big picture" of the whole Bible. These sections are OPTIONAL—only use them if you have time. Remember that it's better to finish in good time having really grasped one big thing from the passage, than to try and cram everything in.

# ⊡ apply

We want to encourage you to spend more time working at application—too often, it is simply tacked on at the end. In the Good Book Guides, apply sections are mixed in with the investigate sections of the study. We hope that people will realise that application is not just an optional extra, but rather, the whole purpose of studying the

Bible. We do Bible study so that our lives can be changed by what we hear from God's word. If you skip the application, the Bible study hasn't achieved its purpose.

These questions draw out practical lessons that we can all learn from the Bible passage. You can review what has been learned so far, and think about practical differences that this should make in our churches and our lives. The group gets the opportunity to talk about what they personally have learned.

# ⊡ getting personal

These can be done at home, but it is well worth allowing a few moments of quiet reflection during the study for each person to think and pray about specific changes they need to make in their own lives. Why not have a time for reporting back at the beginning of the following session, so that everyone can be encouraged and challenged by one another to make application a priority?

# ⬆ pray

In Acts 4 v 25-30 the first Christians quoted Psalm 2 as they prayed in response to the persecution of the apostles by the Jewish religious leaders. Today however, it's not as common for Christians to base prayers on the truths of God's word as it once was. As a result, our prayers tend to be weak, superficial and self-centred rather than bold, visionary and God-centred.

The prayer section is based on what has been learned from the Bible passage. How different our prayer times would be if we were genuinely responding to what God has said to us through His word.

# 1 Genesis 1 and 2
# FOUNDATIONS

## THE BIG IDEA

Man and woman were created equal yet different.

## SUMMARY

Adam and Eve were created by God, in His image, to relate to Him and to rule the world on His behalf. Though equal, they were designed to be different, to complement one another as they ruled God's creation together. Adam was the "head" or leader of the relationship and Eve was his indispensable "helper".

## OPTIONAL EXTRA

Draw up a list of words/titles to read out to your group. You could include the names of films, authors, famous commercial brands, TV programmes, food, hobbies, etc. People in your group need to decide whether they associate each item with men or women. You could keep a tally of how people vote. Use this in conjunction with questions 1 and 2.

**Examples:**

Chocolate

The Bourne trilogy (films)

Sheds

Jane Austen

Sports highlights programme

Shoes

Steak

Apple Store (the shop)

## GUIDANCE FOR QUESTIONS

**1 & 2. What makes men and women fundamentally the same as each other? List some of the similarities you've noticed. Think of some of the ways men and women are different. Do you think we are born with these differences, or do we learn them from the world around us?** (Good for discussing in pairs and then feeding back to the group.)
The following questions may help to get discussion on differences going:

- **In what ways do boys and girls play differently?**
- **In what ways do men and women cope with problems differently?**
- **What different kinds of films do men and women generally choose to watch?**

You can return to these in question 12, to reinforce the Bible's teaching that men and women are equal, yet different, and designed to complement one another.
It might help to draw up a spectrum of masculine to feminine characteristics on a flip chart. It is striking to see that such characteristics (despite inevitably being very generalised) do seem to reflect the purpose for which men and women were made in Genesis 2. For example, the generally male characteristic of being "task-orientated" is well suited to the job given to Adam in Genesis 2 v 15. And the way most women are emotionally and relationally "wired up" also echoes both the first purpose given for the creation of Eve (to be in relationship with Adam, Genesis 2 v 18) and the creation design of women to bear children.

**3. What job description did God give to the first humans (v 28-31)? Is there any**

**difference between men and women here?** Humans were all given the role of displaying God's image, which is only fully reflected in male and female together. They were given the tasks of ruling and reproducing in God's world. No difference between men and women is highlighted in Genesis 1: they are equal in dignity.

**4. In what ways are humans different from the rest of creation (v 24-27)?** Genesis 1 shows that men and women are different from the rest of creation—in their role and responsibility, and in their relationship with God, since uniquely they are made in His image.

**5. What does it mean that we are "created in God's image"? Remember to look at the surrounding verses to help you find an answer.** Much ink has been spilt over what it means to be made in God's image. At the very least it must mean that we can relate to Him in a unique way, unlike the rest of creation. God exists in loving relationship between the three persons of the Trinity—He has made us to relate to one another to reflect this. Also God is the sovereign Ruler—we reflect His image in that we were created to rule earth on His behalf.

**6. APPLY: How does Genesis 1 challenge people and cultures who view and treat women as second-class citizens?** The equal status of men and women in the eyes of God is a very important truth to underline for anyone from a culture where women are seen as inferior to men.

• **What does it say to those who view men as "surplus to requirements"?** In the west, medical developments mean women can have children without finding a male partner; and many children live in homes with no adult men around. This has led to a growing view that men are dispensable. But Genesis 1 shows it is wrong to view men as inferior, just as it is to view women in this way.

**7. What did the man (Adam) spend his time doing before Eve came along? How did he relate to the rest of creation?** Genesis 2 v 4-7, 15-25 shows Adam beginning his life without Eve. Yet verse 18 is striking as, in a world which has been declared "very good" (1 v 31), it is "not good" that Adam's alone. He's incomplete. So Eve is created to meet his need.

**8. Why do you think God parades the animals in front of Adam in search of a helper?** God brings the animals in front of Adam to show that none of them are suitable to meet his need. Only another human being who shares God's image will do.

• **How does Adam's response in v 23 show Eve is the perfect match?** Eve is shown to be equal to him. She, unlike the rest of creation, shares his humanity—she is made of the same "stuff" as Adam (even from his own body) and he sees this with delight—so she can be united to him in "one flesh".

**9. In what ways is Eve shown to be different from Adam, in how, when and why she was created? What do you think is the significance of this?** Eve is equal to Adam; but also different. She is made after Adam; is created out of his body; and is made for the purpose of being his suitable helper. Adam is very much the central character in this chapter and Eve is created as God's gift to him.

**10. What significance is there in the**

fact that Adam names her (2 v 23 and 3 v 20)? The significance of naming in the Bible is that it implies loving authority over, or responsibility for, that which is named (for example, when Adam names the creatures in 2 v 19). The naming of his own wife underlines his loving responsibility for her and his leadership in their relationship.

**11. Summarise what you have learned about the complementary relationship between Adam and Eve. How do verses 24 and 25 show that God's design was good?** Eve perfectly fits Adam and they are "united", like two equally essential, yet differently shaped, pieces of a jigsaw puzzle. Verse 25 sums up the happiness of this pure, harmonious union.

## EXPLORE MORE

Don't get sidetracked onto head covering as you look at this passage. Focus on what is clear, which is that Paul uses Genesis 1 and 2 to show men and women to be equal, and needing each another (v 11-12), yet different in order of responsibility.
**How does Paul help us to understand that men and women are created equal?** Both men and women can pray and prophesy (v 4-5). Men and women are not independent of each other. Both need the other sex (v 11-12). And both come from God (v 12). **And that they are created different?** The man is the "head" of the woman (v 3). Paul picks up on the fact that God deliberately created the woman from the man and created her after him (v 8-9). It is interesting that Paul goes right back to the creation story to teach that it is important to uphold clearly the distinction between men and women in the church family. The specific application to the church to which Paul was writing was that women should continue to cover their heads (this signified

that the women were under the headship of men—or perhaps husbands). They needed to see that having equality in Christ did not mean that they should despise culturally relevant ways to express the headship of men.
**How does Paul describe the relationship between Christ and God (v 3)? How does this help us to understand rightly equality and difference in male-female relationships?** The relationship between men and women reflects the relationship between God and Christ. God is the head of Christ just as the man is the head of the woman. This powerfully underlines the fact that equality between men and women is unaffected by differences in their roles, in the family, the church and the world.

**12. APPLY: How does the complementary design for men and women outlined in Genesis 2 fit your observations in questions 1 and 2?** Your group will need to look back at what was discussed in talkabout—questions 1 and 2. Hopefully they will see how their own observations fit with what they have learned in Genesis 2 about God's design for men and women.

**13. APPLY: God designed women to be different from men. How does that affect the way we see ourselves? How does it encourage and challenge us?** The fact that God has given us a distinct role from men releases us from trying to be like men. We don't have to compete with them or feel either inadequate or superior to them. It allows us to embrace true femininity. Our helper design gives us the dignity and value of being indispensable to men! It also points to our God-given role of helping them to be "real men". We are called to help them be men who:

- take responsibility, rather than abdicating it.
- protect and honour women rather than abusing them.
- take the lead in fulfilling God's purposes in the family, the church and the world.

- **How does it affect the way we see the men we know? How can we encourage them to be responsible and take a godly lead?** We can help and encourage them in this, by giving our full support, energy and prayer, and not by trying to do it for them!

---

## 2 Genesis 3 v 1-24
# WOMEN AND THE FALL

### THE BIG IDEA
At the fall the battle of the sexes begins.

### SUMMARY
At the fall we see both rebellion against God's rule and the overturning of God's created order. This leads to alienation from God and from one another. The relationship between men and women is now subject to pain, confusion and power struggle. Harmony is replaced by shame and distrust. But we can be restored in Christ as we are transformed into His likeness.

### OPTIONAL EXTRA
Hand out a pile of women's magazines (or the kind of pocket guides to "being a successful woman" that can be obtained in most big bookshops). This will help the group to trace how God's design for men and women (the design to be equal, different and complementary) has been distorted since the fall. (This can be used in conjunction with "apply" question 10.)

### GUIDANCE FOR QUESTIONS
**1. Compare the world we live in with the picture of the first man and woman living in perfect harmony in Genesis 2.**

**How do they match up?** Use this question to recap what was learned in the last session.

**2. What tactics did the snake (ie: Satan) use to tempt Eve?** Satan tempts Eve to doubt God's word ("Did God really say...?", v 1), His judgment ("You will not certainly die", v 4) and His character. God is portrayed as a spoilsport: His word cannot be trusted, and He won't carry out His threats. Sin, conversely, seems very attractive, appealing to Eve's appetites ("good for food and pleasing to the eye", v 6) and her pride ("desirable for gaining wisdom", v 6). Sin promises everything.

- **How does he use them still today to tempt people?** Satan's tactics are the same today. Get your group to think about ways they have thought in the past, or the attitudes of non-Christian people they know, which are similar to Eve's thought processes here, in regard to God's word, God's character and what sin promises. It may be helpful to give a scenario involving someone being tempted, eg: to start an affair with a married man; to lie on a school application form; to gossip about a difficult neighbour.

**3. Where does Eve go wrong?** Eve's first mistake is to listen to Satan. Her next mistake is to rely on the character of the snake above the character of God.

- **How do her actions here fall short of the role she is given in Genesis 2 v 18?** She also fails to discuss things with her husband, even though God has made him the leader or "head" in the relationship. (This is illustrated elsewhere in Scripture, especially by Paul, 1 Corinthians 11 v 2-16 and 1 Timothy 2 v 11-15.) She now makes an executive decision to take the fruit and give it to her husband.

**4. Where does Adam go wrong? (Clue: Where was he while Eve was being tempted, v 6?)** Adam is also clearly at fault: he lets Eve go along with Satan's suggestion. It is quite a surprise to see that he "was with her" all along (v 6). Yet instead of jumping to her defence and reminding her of God's command and character, he abdicates his responsibility and lets her make the decision.

**5. Read v 17. How does God hold Adam responsible for the rebellion?** God condemns Adam "because [he] listened to [his] wife and ate fruit from the tree"—v 17. Although Adam tries to blame his wife, God still holds him ultimately responsible as the head, and it will be his name that represents the whole of fallen humanity in the Bible.

- **Why did he make Adam responsible?** God did this to reaffirm His created order—the man is the head of the woman.

**6. How did the fall affect Adam and Eve's relationship with God (v 8-13, 22-24)?** In their relationship with God the consequences of Adam and Eve's sin are fear, dishonesty and shame—they hide from the LORD God (v 8), and they try to keep quiet abut what they have done (v 10). When their actions are exposed, they resort to blaming God ("The woman you put here with me", v 12). The final outcome is banishment from God's presence and so from eternal life (v 22-24).

**7. How did it affect their relationship with each other (v 7, 12, 16)?** In their relationship with one another, the consequences are distrust, buck-passing and disunity (v 12). They now feel they have to cover up (v 7). The relationship between men and women, which is designed to complement perfectly, will instead be confused and fraught with pain (v 16).

**8. How do the curses (v 16-19) reflect the different roles originally given to Adam and Eve? In what way have those roles been spoiled by the fall?** The curses set out for men and women correspond to the roles for which they were created. Having rejected God's purposes for them (which were designed to be for their good), the punishment is that it will now be very hard to fulfil these purposes. The area of work is cursed for the man (v 17-19) and the area of family relationships is cursed for the woman (v 16). She rejects his leadership and seeks to grasp power from him. Conversely, he will "rule over" her with harsh abuse of his authority. It's a far cry from the devoted leadership of loving, protecting, honouring and providing for her, seen in Genesis 2.

## EXPLORE MORE

**What has happened to us if we are Christians (v 10)?** These verses really explain the reason for this course. Christians have been given a new nature—we become new creations in Christ—but that is just the beginning. As new creations we can know the joy of gradually being renewed (changed) into the people we were designed to be—like God. **What does this mean for the curses of Genesis 3?** This means that the effect of the Genesis 3 curses should begin to be reversed in our lives.

**As new people, Paul says, we are "being renewed in knowledge in the image of [our] Creator" (v 10). But how does this actually happen in reality? Have a look at v 15-17 and notice three ways.** In practice, this happens:

• as we live together, at peace with God and with one another (v 15).
• as we use God's word ("message") to learn from, meditate, teach and admonish one another, and celebrate God's goodness with thankfulness (v 16). This means that we need to work hard at the "knowledge" of God's word, through which He teaches us who we are and who we will be. And we need one another— we need to be involved in a church.
• as we make it our aim to glorify Christ and show gratitude to God in everything we say or do (v 17).

**9. APPLY: Think about the battle of the sexes today. How is the equality of the sexes under attack?** There are many ways in which the struggle between the sexes is seen in action. Instead of equality, we have seen the oppression of women down many ages and across cultures. Around the world, we see discrimination, abuse and denial of human rights.

• **How is the difference and complementarity of the sexes under attack?** Elsewhere, the differences between the sexes are being blurred or even rejected, and equality is confused with sameness (for example, in role, vocation, dress).
  • This loss of distinction underlies the increasingly widespread acceptance, even promotion, of homosexuality.
• The complementary design of the sexes has been obscured by a new creed: competition. The western world urges women not just to do what men do but to do it better. This attitude often brings hurt to marriages and family life as women think they need to "have it all".
• Men often sense that they have lost their "role", and indeed, all too many will simply abdicate their responsibility, retreating into the "hen-pecked" category, or, worse, hammering out a "male" identity for themselves in aggression and violence.
• Women are under huge pressure to exercise perhaps the greatest power at their disposal to manipulate men: sex appeal. A generation of teenagers is growing up believing the most important thing about them is how attractive they are to the opposite sex.

Encourage the women not just to assess critically what the world around them is saying, but also to think about how they themselves can so easily buy into the same assumptions and attitudes in their own lives.

**10. APPLY: In what ways might we display this "Genesis 3" way of relating to men? (You might like to think about marriage and/or the workplace.)** The easiest area to discuss is marriage, because God has given differentiated roles for husbands and wives. If there are single women in your group, the marriage aspect will be important in preparing for the future for some of these women, and also in enabling them to helpfully support married friends. (Marriage will be covered in more detail in the next session.) However, discussion of relationships with men as colleagues will probably be more immediately relevant to single women. It's important to note that Genesis chapters 1 – 3 do not contain teaching that is explicitly directed towards work relationships between men and women (although more directly applicable guidelines can be found in other parts of Scripture, eg: Ephesians 6 v 5-9). The question of the extent to which complementary gender roles assigned by God within marriage also apply to male/female relationships in other contexts (eg: paid employment, politics, community institutions) remains a grey area among Bible-believing Christians. However, we can see that the attitudes of women to men (and vice versa) in the workplace will undoubtedly have been affected by the fall and the resulting battle of the sexes. Working women may find it illuminating to think about differences in the way they may treat male as opposed to female subordinates, or how they respond to a male as opposed to a female boss, or how they react to the promotion of a male equal as opposed to a female one.

Re-cap what is meant by a "Genesis 3" way of relating to men—rejecting male leadership and seeking to grasp power for ourselves. This might include depriving men of initiative by seizing it for ourselves; undermining men, damaging their ability to lead; manipulating men into following our agenda (by using our sexuality, by nagging, by playing the martyr, etc).

## 3 Matthew 19; Ephesians 5; Proverbs 31
# WOMEN AND MARRIAGE

### THE BIG IDEA
God designed marriage to glorify Him. He is glorified as the husband and wife mirror Christ's relationship with the church.

### SUMMARY
Marriage was designed by God and its purpose is to mirror the love between Christ and the church. For the wife, it requires wholehearted commitment to living out the helper design in marriage. This results in blessing that reaches beyond the marriage, to those around.

**Note:** It is worthwhile making the point that the Bible's teaching on marriage can, and must, have application to single people, not least because all married people start out as single people! It is vital to gain a clear understanding of God's design for how husband and wife relate within marriage, before getting married. When choosing a partner, it is good to seek a husband who would be a joy to submit to and whose godly lead can be trusted and followed. Women need to be prepared to enter a marriage as a "helper suitable for him".

**Pastoral note:** This can be a very painful topic for those who are unmarried, or unhappily married. Sensitivity may be needed on the part of the group leader.

It is very likely that during this study discussion will turn to the question of divorce. Be aware that those who have been touched by divorce, either as adults or children, may find this a painful subject to discuss, and you will need to be sensitive in how you handle the discussion. We must be firm on what God has said in His word, but compassionate for those who struggle with the pain of this issue.

Divorce is permitted in the Bible (Deuteronomy 24 v 1-4); but Jesus makes clear that God only allows divorce in order to deal with the effects of sin—because "your hearts were hard" (Matthew 19 v 8). Divorce is always the result of sin (though not necessarily by both partners). It was "not this way from the beginning": to God, divorce is always a tragedy because it undoes something that God has done (v 6).

The Lord Jesus is clear that the only acceptable reason for divorce is marital unfaithfulness (v 9); Paul adds that if an unbelieving spouse leaves someone who is a Christian, then the Christian is "not bound" (1 Corinthians 7 v 15).

It is always worth reminding your group that Jesus loves us despite our past (not because of it), and has died for all the wrongdoing in our lives (see for example 1 Corinthians 6 v 9-11). If anyone is considering divorce, encourage them to allow God to speak to them in His word, to pray hard about it, and to seek counsel from a Christian pastor.

A related issue is remarriage. Christians disagree on when remarriage is pleasing to God. Widows can remarry (1 Corinthians 7 v 39). Those who have been active in getting divorced (ie: were willing to accept a divorce, rather than having it forced upon them by their ex-spouse leaving the marriage) should not (Matthew 19 v 9), unless their ex-spouse was maritally unfaithful. Clearly, there are some grey areas here, and it would be wise to acknowledge them as such.

## OPTIONAL EXTRA

Find some quotations on marriage (easily found on the internet). Read through them with your group and discuss what popular views of marriage they portray. Eg:
"Marriage is a great institution, but I'm not ready for an institution." (Mae West)
"Bachelors know more about women than married men; if they didn't, they'd be married too." (H.L. Mencken)
"Brought up to respect the conventions, love had to end in marriage. I'm afraid it did." (Bette Davis)
"A man doesn't know what happiness is until he is married. By then it is too late." (Frank Sinatra)

## GUIDANCE FOR QUESTIONS

**1. In some western countries, only half of all marriages survive. What makes marriage so hard? How can you trace this back to Genesis 3?** In discussing what makes marriage hard, you might like to go back to the discussion in the last session. The fall affects marriage because sin ruins relationships, and because it has shaped society's distorted view of manhood and womanhood.

**2. List five things from [Matthew 19 v 4-6] that make up a marriage.** (See also Mark 10 v 6-9.) Jesus affirms God's plan for marriage and quotes the pattern established in creation (Genesis 2 v 23-24). Marriage is heterosexual ("male and female"), public ("leave his father and mother"), faithful and sexual ("one flesh"), permanent ("let no one separate") and God-joined ("God has joined together"). (Of course your group may express these things differently.)

- **How does this compare to our culture's view of what makes a marriage?** Of course, marriage customs differ between cultures. Western culture's obsession with "being in love" as the number one requirement for marriage is not found in Scripture! But the command to love your spouse is.

**3. Re-read Genesis 1 v 26-28 and 2 v 18. What is marriage for? Compare this to our culture's view.** The purpose of marriage in Genesis is primarily partnership in doing God's work in His world (partly through peopling it!). This contrasts with the world's view of marriage being for our personal happiness.

**4. What does it mean for a wife to submit (v 22-24, 33)?** It is surprising to find in Ephesians 5 v 22-33 that both a wife's submission and a husband's love are pretty comprehensive. The wife's submission should look like the church's obedience to Christ (although clearly it should not draw a wife away from obedience to Christ). "Submission" is hardly a politically-correct term these days; but it does not imply inequality for wives any more than it did for Christ. He, though equal with the Father as fully God, gladly and freely accepted His different role in the relationship and submitted to His Father.

- **We've seen that an aspect of being a "helper" is actively to enable and encourage a husband's leadership. How does this tie in with that?** It is worth unpacking what submission looks like (in action and attitude). It's important to underline that submission is not a passive response to the husband's role, but reflects the church's submission to Christ of actively seeking His interests and following His lead. A wife is called to be the strong "helper" of Genesis 2.

**Note:** Verse 21, "Submit to one another

out of reverence for Christ", has caused many to say that this must mean that a husband is to submit to his wife in the same way that a wife submits to her husband. Verse 21 introduces a whole section on submission in the letter, calling on believers to submit to the appropriate people in the appropriate contexts. But Paul is not inviting the conclusion that everyone should submit to everyone else in the same way. If this were so, we would have to say that parents must obey children and masters are to obey slaves (compare chapter 6). Paul simply doesn't say in verse 21 that husbands are to submit to wives.

**5. What should a husband's love look like (v 25-30)? Why?** Husbands have at least as much demanded of them in this section. To imitate Christ's self-sacrificing love for the church is no small order. Like Christ's goal for the church, his goal for his wife must be her holiness and he is to look after her wellbeing, just as he looks after his. It is worth fleshing out this love with practical implications; for example, how a husband can encourage his wife to grow in holiness.

**6. How does v 32 motivate a husband and wife to work hard at their roles in marriage?** The spiritual meaning of marriage is highlighted in verse 32. It is all about reflecting the "profound mystery" of the union between Christ and His bride, the church. God had Christ and the church in mind when He invented marriage.

**7. APPLY: How could this passage be used to help a Christian marriage that is struggling?** God's purpose for Christian marriage—to reflect the unity and relationship of Christ and His church— should be a powerful motivation for a husband/wife to start living out the role within marriage that God has assigned to them. If a husband or wife is not motivated to adopt these roles by God's higher purpose for marriage outlined here, then that would indicate that there is another problem—a spiritual or theological one—which needs to be addressed.

**8. APPLY: How could this passage help shape what a single person might look for in a husband, or what they might seek to be as a wife?** A single woman will need to look for a man that she is happy to submit to and can trust to look after her wellbeing in every area, including her growth in holiness. A single man will need to look for a woman that he is able to love with a Christlike love, and can lead.

## EXPLORE MORE
**How does Peter advise these women in v 1-2? What encouragement does he offer?** Clearly not all marriages portray this relationship effectively, especially where one partner is not a believer. In 1 Peter 3, Peter encourages wives to fulfil their role, regardless of whether a husband believes or is fulfilling his role. In doing so, a believing wife is in the best position to win her husband for Christ. Her godly character and submission will be far more effective than preaching at him.
**Pastoral note:** Sadly, some marriages (even Christian ones) are highly abusive. Submission does not mean doing nothing. It may be appropriate to take action to ensure the wellbeing of a wife, children and even an abusive husband. It is still possible for a wife to have a loyal, respectful attitude towards her husband as her head, to whom she is committed as his helper, while involving appropriate church or state authorities. In extreme cases (for example,

for the sake of safety), this may involve having an attitude of loyalty to a husband, while physically separated from him. It is the responsibility of the church family to exercise a great deal of pastoral wisdom, care and support.

**9. What are this woman's roles and responsibilities, both inside and outside the home?** Proverbs 31 v 10-31 fleshes out what a godly wife looks like. Her priorities are her husband and children (v 11-12, 15, 21, 26-28), yet her care and compassion extend beyond her own family (v 20). She is hard-working (v 15, 17, 18, 27), and a wise businesswoman (v 13, 16, 18, 24).

• **How is she fulfilling the role of "helper" to her husband here?** Her husband is free from worrying about the running of the family home, so is able to focus on his own responsibilities (v 23).

**10. What kinds of attitudes and priorities do you think give her a "noble" character in God's eyes?** The climax of this description comes in v 29-30. God views her character as noble because she fears Him. Despite her wide-ranging responsibilities and skills, she has a godly perspective on life.

• **Why is she worth "far more than rubies" to her husband?** Rubies might bring status, but money can't buy fear of the LORD (v 30), or the wisdom and faithful instruction that comes from that (v 26), or the sense of security that comes from knowing God (v 25). She truly is "blessed" (v 28).

**11. APPLY: What can we learn from the woman of Proverbs 31 today...**
• **for living out the helper design within**

**marriage?** The woman of Proverbs 31 teaches that a woman can fulfil her helper role in marriage by:

- making the running of the home and family her priority, despite having many other responsibilities.
- working at her tasks with eagerness, thoughtfulness, faithfulness and diligence.
- cultivating fear of the LORD, generosity, peace about the future, wisdom, faithful instruction and watchfulness.

- **for all women, married or single, who want to be women of noble character?** We can learn from this woman that above all we must fear the LORD.

# 4 1 Corinthians 7 v 1-9, 25-40
# WOMEN AND SINGLENESS

## THE BIG IDEA
Singleness is a good gift from the ultimate Husband.

## SUMMARY
Singleness may be seen negatively in society, and even the church, but it is a good gift from God, to be used for His glory. It comes with many practical advantages in serving God in a world that urgently needs the gospel. The greatest encouragement for single people is to know that Christ is the perfect Husband.

## OPTIONAL EXTRA
Talk about a woman who used her gift of singleness to serve the Lord. Dr. Helen Roseveare is a good, contemporary example: she at one stage considered but finally gave up the prospect of marriage, though not without a struggle (see her autobiography, *Give me this mountain*, p111-116). After her first term as a medical missionary in Congo, she started thinking about getting married before returning to Africa, despite recognising that marriage would have restricted her freedom to do some of the things she had done in her first term. She set out to win a particular Christian man. However, he did not feel called to overseas missionary service. She started to think about giving up her work in the Congo for marriage. The struggle between her desire for marriage and her vocation finally ended with both of them agreeing to give up meeting one another. Other details of Dr. Roseveare's life and achievements in Christian missionary service can easily be found on the internet.

## GUIDANCE FOR QUESTIONS
**1. How does our society view singleness? Include both positive and negative images.** In society and in the church, singleness can be viewed both positively and negatively. In western society, singleness can be seen as giving freedom, (though usually sexual freedom is what is meant). If singleness means celibacy, it is often portrayed as negative and also (often in the media) as something to be ashamed of.

- **What kinds of views do Christians have on singleness?** In the church, singleness and celibacy go together where people are submitting to God's word. Yet there can still be something of a stigma attached to it. Phrases like "on the shelf" are all too frequently used to describe singleness. Some churches place so much emphasis on supporting family life that they unwittingly neglect those who are unmarried. Equally, singleness can be seen as "super-spiritual", somehow lifting Christians onto some fictional higher level of commitment to the Lord.

Discussing the different ways that your group have seen these attitudes expressed will help identify any wrong thinking.

**2. This world could end at any time (v 29-31). How should that affect the way we see our lives, single or married? How does it affect our approach to time, priorities, money and ambitions?**
The context of Paul's teaching on singleness and marriage in 1 Corinthians 7 is that "this world in its present form is passing away" (v 31). Time is short and so the priority for every Christian is to look to "the Lord's affairs"—the growth of His kingdom. This means that neither singleness nor marriage is the be-all and end-all of life for Christians. You might like to use the following questions to prompt discussion on the specific areas outlined:

• **Time:** In your weekly schedule, apart from your job, what time have you set aside for church meetings; personal Bible reading and prayer; meeting with other Christians; meeting with non-Christians who you pray for and seek to witness to.

• **Priorities:** Do you fit your (or your family's) social life and leisure activities around church and other Christian responsibilities—or the other way round?

• **Money:** Do you give regularly and consistently to any Christian work? Do you work out your Christian giving along with other essential financial commitments, or do you look at what's left after you have

spent on everything else?

• **Ambitions:** What is the most important thing you want to achieve before you die? What is the most important thing you want for those closest to you? What is your aim for each day when you get up?

**3. Verse 7 tells us that both marriage and singleness are gifts from God. How should this change the way you see your situation?** Everyone has a gift from God regarding their marital state: either singleness, or marriage. Paul is not commenting on how much we enjoy our particular gift. He is simply encouraging an attitude of seeing that all we are is from God, and is therefore to be received and used with thankfulness.

**4. Compare our romantic ideals with what Paul says about marriage (v 28). What kinds of troubles do you think he has in mind?** Your group will probably be able to talk about marriage troubles from personal experience and observations (but do remind people to honour confidences). You could point out that in addition, Christians in Paul's day also faced opposition and persecution. Those with spouses and/ or children had to consider the effect of making a stand for Christ on their families.

**5. How do Paul's views on singleness (v 32-35) differ from the way we often think about it?** Paul majors on the advantages of being single above marriage. This is quite a surprise to the majority of Christians, who naturally tend to think the opposite, and it is worth spending time discussing this with the group. He is not making a negative judgement on the naturally and rightly "divided" interests of the married person in 1 Corinthians 7, but merely stating the fact that this is so.

**6. What does it mean for a single person to be "devoted to the Lord in both body and spirit" (v 34)? Why does being unmarried make a difference (v 32)?** The advantages for a Christian in being single are practical more than anything else. A single person often has more freedom, under God, to decide where they will spend their time and emotional energy.

**7. APPLY: List the things that single people can enjoy and ways they can serve, which they couldn't do if they were married.** This question provides a chance to counteract the teaching of the world, which often suggests singleness is second best. Getting our heads around the great advantages of singleness, and the possibilities for serving God that this gift provides, is greatly encouraging. Single people have a gift to use; they are not simply those lacking the gift of marriage.

• **How can you and your church best support and encourage single people?** Ideas for discussion include: families adopting single people, so they can enjoy aspects of family life that they may otherwise miss out on eg: family meals, contact with children; looking out for single people at tricky times of year eg: Christmas and New Year, Mother's Day, summer holidays; making an effort to encourage single people in their service for the Lord, etc.

## EXPLORE MORE
**How do [the following passages] help us to understand this eternal perspective on marriage and singleness?**
• **Ephesians 5 v 25-31:** Jesus alone has been the perfect Husband in His sacrificial death on the cross for us, calling us back to Himself, forgiving, restoring and comforting us, and making us beautiful for Him.
• **Mark 12 v 25:** Marriage in this world is only a preview of the true marriage of God's people with our Saviour. Once we are in the full reality of that marriage, the earthly symbol of it will no longer be needed.
• **Isaiah 54 v 4-8 and Revelation 21 v 1-4:** For those who struggle with singleness and long for marriage, it is wonderfully encouraging to know that, as Christians, we already have the "real thing" in Christ, and our betrothal to Him will soon be fully consummated in heaven. We can guarantee that no one will look back then and still think that they were missing out!

**8. APPLY: Write down three things that can encourage you in your relationship with [Jesus]—both now and in the future.** This truth that Jesus Christ is our ultimate Husband is precious to every believer, especially in the light of how hard both marriage and singleness can sometimes be.

# 5 1 Peter 3; 1 Timothy 2
# WOMEN AND BEAUTY

## THE BIG IDEA
Beauty according to the world is very different from true beauty according to the word.

## SUMMARY
Outward beauty can easily become an idol for women. A godly approach to it involves obeying the biblical standards of modesty, decency and appropriate dress. It also involves pursuing godly inner beauty and good deeds, in preference to being concerned about our appearance.

## OPTIONAL EXTRA
You could have some fun by investigating changing standards of beauty through the ages. Internet sites that give image results for this are:
www.hubpages.com/hub/Standards_of_Be auty_An_Illustrated_Timeline
www.ukhairdressers.com/history%20of%2 0beauty.asp
www.maysstuff.com/womenid.htm
For weird and wonderful, sometimes scary beauty tips used by ancient Egyptians, Elizabethans, Victorians and in various decades of the 20th century see:
www.groovygames.com/hinge/bathstuff/b eauty/beauty.html
One point that this will underline is the fickleness of standards of beauty. Aiming at being beautiful is like firing at a moving target. Beauty can never be a goal in life that brings complete satisfaction.

## GUIDANCE FOR QUESTIONS
**1. Women today are under enormous pressure to look beautiful. How does this pressure affect our society?** Once again, the use of women's magazines might prompt some good discussion. The pressure on women to be beautiful is undoubtedly enormous, fuelling a multi-million-pound industry. The effects have been quite devastating, from the huge rise in eating disorders to the abuse of women's bodies as sex objects.

• **What are the effects in your own life?**

**2. What should not be the source of our beauty (v 3)? Why not?** Peter is not saying that physical beauty is to be scorned. Other parts of Scripture celebrate beauty. But he is saying that it is not primarily where our beauty should "come from". Rather than pouring all our energies into what we look like, we should recognise and seek first "the unfading beauty of a gentle and quiet spirit" (v 4).

Notice that it is in the context of submitting to husbands that Peter addresses the issue of the way we dress. Submission (in the church family) is also the context for Paul's teaching on the outward appearance in 1 Timothy 2 and 1 Corinthians 11. It seems that the way we dress says a lot about how we view our husbands and brothers. The power of our appearance is arguably the greatest power women can have over men. If we are fulfilling our helper design, we will not want to use that power over them.

**3. Where should our beauty come from? How is it connected to our relationship with God (v 2-5)?** True beauty that lasts and pleases God has its roots in a secure relationship with Him. It belongs to women who revere and "put their hope in [him]" (v 5)—who know that what He sees is what counts (v 4).

**4. Describe what such a character ("gentle and quiet") would look like.** "A gentle and quiet spirit" describes a woman who is at peace because of her assurance of God's love for her. She is quieted by His love (see Zephaniah 3 v 17 in the ESV or NIV1984)—secure, contented, with nothing to prove and no axe to grind. Such beauty won't cry out for attention and admiration, but be gentle in manner, providing a place of safety for others. Jesus uses this same word for "gentle" in Matthew 11 v 29.

• **What would the opposite look like?** The opposite is a woman who is not secure in the knowledge of God's love for her. Instead of trusting absolutely in all that Christ has done to win for her forgiveness and acceptance from God, she feels she has to earn His approval and impress Him (or others). She may be very driven, judgmental of others, discontented and complaining, needy and a drain on others, cynical and distrustful, or resentful and rebellious.

**5. APPLY: What will help us to cultivate the true beauty of "a gentle and quiet spirit"?** "A gentle and quiet spirit" shows we are secure in the love of God in Christ. This security comes from knowing and understanding the truth of the gospel about Jesus Christ (Romans 5 v 8). Get your group to discuss how they can speak the gospel to each other more, and encourage each other to live in the light of what Christ has done for us.

**6. What does it mean to dress with modesty, decency and propriety (which means appropriateness)? What does our**

**culture think of such qualities?** Contrary to what our culture says, the way Christian women dress must not be extravagant, showy or sexually manipulative. Our choice of clothing should be influenced by the need to help one another live to glorify God, and to understand His word. We don't want people to give us all the attention but to discover Jesus Christ. We don't want people to desire us but to desire to hear what God says.

**7. Why do you think Paul calls Christian women to be like this?** To dress in a way that flouts modesty, decency and propriety would both undermine the fact that we worship a holy God, and be very unloving towards our brothers (and sisters).

• **What will it mean for us in practice?** The decisions we take regarding what and what not to wear as a woman of God will vary according to the culture we live in. Areas for discussion could include: sexually unhelpful clothes; slogans; clothes that intimidate others.

**8. Why is it inappropriate for "women who profess to worship God" to let our appearance devour our time, thoughts and money?** Our preoccupation is to be the worship of God, not an obsession with what we look like. That would point to an idol rather than the true God. It would suggest that His life-changing power hasn't made any difference to us and that our insecurities remain the same as the rest of the world's.

• **What makes good deeds (v 10) a woman's best accessory?** Good deeds enhance and draw attention to true beauty, the "gentle and quiet spirit" that is of great worth in God's sight. It is when we trust and hope in God that we can give up serving our own interests and passions, and instead devote ourselves to the good of others. So good deeds highlight the very different way in which Christians are able to live as they respond to God's grace.

## EXPLORE MORE

**What things are mentioned in these verses that will help us to beautify our lives with good deeds?** These verses from Hebrews 10 give pointers about how to help ourselves and each other to be devoted to good deeds.

- **Verse 19-23:** True good deeds don't come from trying to win God's acceptance by impressing Him with our goodness—they come from the response of our grateful hearts to the life, forgiveness, cleansing and hope that God freely and graciously gives to us in Jesus Christ.

- **Verse 24-25:** We need each other to spur one another to show love and do good deeds. That means we should be joined to a community of Christians; we need to keep meeting together; and when we meet, we need to be active in encouraging each other.

**Note:** The key to the following application questions is to get people to think honestly and practically. However, it is important that people don't go away with a list of dos and don'ts about how to dress. Rather, we need primarily to develop a greater appreciation of what is truly beautiful and a commitment to pursuing that above outward beauty. Modesty, decency and propriety will flow out of that.

**9. APPLY: How do we need to re-shape our understanding of what beauty is?** Get people to compare what they have learned about true beauty with the popular understanding of beauty in our culture. God's view of true beauty may well be obvious to everyone in your group but the big question is: which understanding of beauty is the one that most affects you in everyday life?

**10. APPLY: How can we pursue true, unfading beauty for ourselves, and encourage others in that pursuit too?** Discuss things that we should stop and things we should start doing. Useful areas of discussion include: unhelpful influences eg: magazines, TV programmes; why we compliment people; how we talk about or describe others; the time and money we devote to our looks or to our growth in godliness.

**11. APPLY: How can we appreciate external appearance without making an idol of it?** The key here is an attitude of thankfulness to our Creator God—the one who has given us beauty, design, colour, imagination and creativity (see 1 Timothy 4 v 4-5). This will protect us from pride, envy and idolatry.

# 6 Galatians 3 – 4; 1 Timothy 2
# WOMEN AND THE FAMILY OF GOD

## THE BIG IDEA

Women have a vital role in the family of God, in which God wants His design for manhood and womanhood to be reflected.

## SUMMARY

Throughout the history of God's people, women have had a vital role to play, and continue to do so. However, some roles of teaching and leadership are reserved for men, in order to reflect the way God has designed men and women to complement, and not duplicate, each other.

## OPTIONAL EXTRA

Get your group to think of all the different kinds of service that are needed in a church and write a list on a whiteboard or flip chart. Think of background, weekday ministries as well as up-front, Sunday ones. Think of all the things that make your church a place where all kinds of people are welcomed in and find a community where they hear God's truth, are saved, are cared for and disciplined, grow in faith and godliness, and are equipped to take the message of the gospel to others. The aim of this activity is to show the abundance of ministries that a Christian can do, of which only a very few are not open to women, and including some that only women can do. (Use this activity in conjunction with apply questions 8 and 9, and with Explore More.)

## GUIDANCE FOR QUESTIONS

**1. List at least ten of the key men and women of God you can think of** from the Bible. What kinds of roles did they have? Did the roles differ at all between men and women? Male headship is the pattern given throughout the Bible, as we see in the fact that it is men who hold the leadership positions of, for example, prophets, priests and kings. In the New Testament, although Jesus never commented directly on the subject, He implicitly endorsed this as God's design for His people when He appointed twelve male apostles. It is helpful to see that Paul, two of whose letters this study is focussing on, doesn't just start talking about a distinction between male and female roles out of nowhere.

**Note:** At some stage in this session, someone may well ask: "What about Deborah?" She appears in Judges 4 and 5 and seems to be an exception to the general rule of male headship in the Bible. Again, her example is not enough upon which to build a whole case for female leadership in the church, especially since her role as judge was in prophesying and settling disputes between individuals. When a national problem arose (4 v 6-7), God appointed a man, Barak. If anything the story reinforces, rather than contradicts, the pattern of male headship in the people of God. And Deborah is a true "helper" to Barak, encouraging his leadership, rather than trying to take it from him.

**2. What is at the heart of the equality described in 3 v 26-29 and 4 v 6-7?** This passage is frequently quoted by "evangelical feminists", who suggest it supports giving men and women equal ministry opportunities in the church. However, in this passage Paul is speaking about salvation and our equal status as heirs of God, whether male or female. We cannot make the phrase "no difference" (eg: Romans 3 v 22) a general statement about men and women. That would contradict what Paul says elsewhere about the importance of different roles for men and women (eg: 1 Timothy 2).

• **Why would this teaching have been so shocking in that culture?** Paul's teaching here would have been radical in a culture where women had no rights of inheritance.

**3. These verses are often used to argue for equal ministry opportunities for men and women in the church. Do you think this can be argued from the passage? Why, or why not?** The main problem with such arguments is that they view equality as meaning "sameness". We need to unlearn this teaching that is so ingrained in us, and look afresh at the Bible's understanding of equality, which embraces difference, not sameness. We see this not only in God's design for men and women, but ultimately in the Godhead, in Jesus, who though "in very nature God, did not consider equality with God something to be used to his own advantage; rather, he made himself nothing" (Philippians 2 v 6-7). Equality of status does not have to mean sameness in role, either in the Godhead or in human relationships.

**4. APPLY: How could you use this teaching to help [women who struggle with insecurity] and introduce them to the gospel?** These verses show the radical difference that faith in Christ will make to

everyday lives. Those who are treated as second-class citizens—whether because of their sex, ethnicity or social class—can find that view of themselves transformed by the truth of what we become and receive in Christ through faith in Him. Even though our situations don't alter, our feelings about ourselves can be totally changed by the truth of the gospel. Having shown these differences, these verses lead you quite easily into explaining the gospel.

**5. What attitude are women to have when they meet together with the church family (v 11-12)?** This passage really grates against everything our own culture tells us to be! Women are not to make sure they have a voice but are to be "quiet" and learn in "quietness and full submission" (v 11). This is set out in contrast to teaching and having authority over men (v 12). As later verses show (3 v 2 and 5 v 17), teaching God's word is an essential part of exercising authority in the church, since the Bible is the only authority for God's people. Therefore, it seems that for a woman to teach men in the gathered assembly of the church would be in some sense an exercise of authority or headship which God has reserved for men. This is reinforced by the fact that Paul specifically addresses men when discussing potential overseers and elders in chapter 3 (even though he still clearly values the role of women—v 11). **Note:** The instruction to women to be quiet (v 12)—or "silent" in some translations— seems to be in the context of teaching and exercising authority over men, rather than an absolute prohibition on women speaking in church meetings. For example, in 1 Corinthians 11, where Paul is also giving instructions about meeting as a church, he assumes that women can pray or prophesy in the gathering of God's people.

**6. What two reasons are given in verses 13-14? Why do you think Paul goes right back to Genesis?** It is worth noting that Paul doesn't refer to the culture of the time, or the specific situation in that church, as the reason for women to let men take on the primary responsibility of teaching and leading of the church. He refers right back to God's creation design and uses what happened at the fall to show the consequences of rejecting that design. Paul sees the significance of the fact that God created the man first, thus giving him primary responsibility (v 13). He also sees the significance of the fact that it was the woman who was approached by the Deceiver (not at all implying that the man wasn't just as guilty!). It was the woman who took on the responsibility to make this momentous decision to disobey God on behalf of her husband and head, while Adam "submitted" to her leadership. The disastrous consequences of stepping outside God's design should drive home the point that women need to allow and encourage men to be men in fulfilling their God-given role of leading and teaching God's people.

**7. APPLY: What will it mean for us to be "women" in the church rather than "men"? What kind of women does v 15 say we should be?** Women need to learn from Eve's example and not assume that they can take on the role God assigned to men, without harmful consequences. In fact they will be "saved" (v 15) from this by embracing true womanhood and all that involves. Childbearing, the most obvious aspect of womanhood, as distinct from manhood, can be taken as shorthand for "being a woman", rather than a literal requirement. Get your group to consider which attitudes shown by women are helpful to male leadership in church, and

which are destructive or subversive.

## EXPLORE MORE

**Look up the following passages and write down all the different ways women serve God in the Bible.** These passages highlight the vast range of ministries carried out by women in the Bible, giving inspiration for women's ministry today. We see that women play a vital role in the family of God.

- **Exodus 15:** Songwriter, musician, song-leader.
- **Proverbs 31:** Charity (v 20), personal, informal teaching and training, especially in the home (v 26-27).
- **John 4:** Telling others about Jesus.
- **Acts 1:** Praying together.
- **Acts 16:** Hospitality.
- **Acts 18:** Private instruction of the preacher Apollos, as part of a married couple.
- **Romans 16:** Several women are commended for their hard work in the Lord, showing the very high value Paul placed on the ministry of women as "fellow workers" for the gospel. Phoebe was a "deacon" or "servant" of the church in Cenchrea. We know from Acts 6 that deacons were set apart for practical and charitable work in the church. It is very likely then that there were deacons in the early church who held this kind of role.
- **1 Timothy 5:** "Good deeds" including bringing up children, hospitality, serving other Christians, helping those in trouble.
- **2 Timothy 1 and 3:** Teaching the Bible and modelling Christian faith to children.
- **Titus 2:** Training younger women to be godly in their everyday lives.

**8. APPLY: How can women serve in your church? How does this complement the way the men serve?** It is helpful to see the broad spectrum of ministries, from catering or welcoming to sharing testimony or helping lead a Bible-study group, as being among the hundreds of ways of serving God and the gospel. This keeps us from devaluing some forms of service as less "spiritual". It is also good to see what women uniquely bring to the church family, which complements what men bring. In the next session we will look more at the teaching ministry open to every godly woman: to get alongside and encourage other women.

**9. APPLY: How would you go about forming opinions in the "grey area"?** You may find it helpful to draw out on a flip chart a broad spectrum of ministries, from those which involve the teaching and leading of the whole church to the more small-scale or practical ministries (see Optional Extra). You could then highlight those responsibilities reserved for men, those clearly open for everyone, and those that fall into a grey area where different Christians and different churches hold different opinions. Some of these areas may include teaching mixed fellowship/home groups, teaching the youth group, leading services, serving as a member of the church council or eldership team and so on. Encourage healthy debate about where to "draw the line", as well as a respect for other people's consciences and opinions (see Romans 14), and some allowance for different church contexts and cultures around the world.

**10. APPLY: How can you develop an attitude of support and willing submission towards church leaders and teachers?** Support of and submission to church leaders is an attitude we are all called to cultivate for mutual benefit (Hebrews 13 v 17). Reflect particularly from 1 Timothy 2 on how that challenges us as women and how we can fulfil our true helper design in the church.

# 7 Titus 2 v 1-5
# WOMEN AND THEIR SISTERS

## THE BIG IDEA
Women should develop friendships with other women, both older and younger, for training and encouragement.

## SUMMARY
The teaching and training of younger women to live out the word of God should happen in the context of learning from godly older women in the church family. Christ-centred friendships with other women should be pursued and made the most of as a great source of blessing and encouragement.

## OPTIONAL EXTRA
You could package this session as something of a "girly" get-together and do some "girly" things. Enjoy being women together; but point out that there is more to friendship between sisters in Christ than this, and such friendship can and should be of much more lasting significance.

## GUIDANCE FOR QUESTIONS
**1. Think about your friendships with men and women. How do they differ? What do you value about friendship**

**with other women?** Without taking anything away from the value of friendships with men, woman-to-woman friendships bring with them the particular blessing of being able to understand where each other is coming from! Similarly, older women, rather than older men, present a more natural role-model for younger women.

**2. Think about an older Christian woman who has influenced you. How did her friendship or example help you?** To kick-start the discussion, be ready with your own example of an older Christian woman that you look up to.

**3. What qualities should an older woman be taught to cultivate (v 3)? What should be her attitude towards God, others and herself?** Paul is instructing Titus on what to teach to the different groups in the church. It is interesting that the only group he isn't told to teach is the younger women. This is to be done by the older women. These verses answer anyone who complains that the Bible does not allow women to teach. Clearly, women have a vital teaching ministry, in teaching one another. It is their responsibility to train the younger women in godliness as they teach and live out God's word alongside them. To be qualified to do this, they need to show a right attitude of reverence to God, love for others and self-control towards themselves.

**4. What areas are highlighted as the focus for the older women in training younger women? Why are these highlighted, do you think?** The training for younger women in verses 4-5 seems to centre on the home, the list beginning and ending with the woman's relationship to her husband. For Christian women who are married, this points to the necessity of right and godly priorities—putting husband, children and the management of home life before career or leisure pursuits. This is not to say that a wife and mother shouldn't work or have any life outside the home (see the working wife of noble character in Proverbs 31). This is liberating teaching for the many women in our culture who feel under pressure to maintain a career while bringing up a family.

**Note:** Single women were rare when Paul wrote, but that doesn't mean that this passage has no application for them. 1 Timothy 5 shows us that although a woman's primary responsibility is to her own family (v 4 and 16), she is also to be devoted to the church family and "all kinds of good deeds" (v 10).

- **How do you think this kind of training can best take place?** We tend to think of teaching in the formal context of classes and courses. But it's likely that the kind of woman-to-woman training outlined here will be most effective in the context of a close relationship, meeting up in each others' homes, taking the frequent opportunities for biblical encouragement, advice and problem-solving alongside prayer.

**5. What will be the result of this kind of training?** The result of such training aims to be that "no one will malign the word of God" (v 5). The joyful living out of God's good design in everyday life is a powerfully attractive witness to non-Christians, and deprives opponents of the gospel of one of their favourite weapons against Christians— the charge of hypocrisy. How Christian women conduct themselves in the home is not an insignificant matter.

## EXPLORE MORE
**Look back to Proverbs 31 v 10-31. How**

**does the wife of noble character flesh out Titus 2 v 3-5? How do you imagine her being an "older woman", involved in the training of younger women? What would they have learned from her?** The wife of Proverbs 31 is the living embodiment of the qualities listed by Paul in Titus 2 v 4-5. This woman's example in everyday life would be great training for the daughters and women servants who see her in action. But we also know that she speaks with wisdom and gives faithful instruction (v 26). Given all her other activities and the culture of the time, this is unlikely to have been in any formal setting.

**6. APPLY: In what kinds of contexts can such woman-to-woman training go on? What are the opportunities for this in your church family?** Get your group to think of ways in which they could set up older/younger women partnerships in your church. For example: a prayer partnership (or triplet); a pre-school group, which older women can be encouraged to join to befriend and help younger mums; a scheme to encourage hospitality for students, singles or senior citizens and even "adopt" someone into your family; a women's Bible-study group.

**7. APPLY: Who are you an "older woman" to? How can you encourage this younger woman, by your example and words, to live a godly life?**

• **Who are you a "younger woman" to? How can you learn from this older woman's words and example to you?** The beauty of Titus 2 is that although Paul probably had in mind a recognised group of "older" godly women in the church, we can all find friendships where we are either the younger or the older woman. Even a woman in her early twenties can be an older woman

to a teenager looking for a role-model. The challenge is to accept that we have a responsibility to those "younger" (in years or in spiritual maturity) than us, and to seek to be worthy of being a role-model for them. Similarly, we need to have the humility to look for "older" role-models to learn from, whatever stage we are at!

## EXPLORE MORE

**What kind of qualities is God looking for in friendships between believers?**

• **Proverbs 12 v 18:** Wise, healing speech, not reckless words.

• **13 v 20:** Friendships with people who are wise, not keeping company with foolish people.

• **17 v 17:** Loyalty through bad times.

• **27 v 5-6:** Being ready to say difficult things that need to be said.

• **27 v 9:** Good and trustworthy advice.

• **27 v 17:** Aiming to improve each other.

**8. APPLY: How can you develop your friendships with other women to include the qualities discussed in Explore More above? Think practically and write down three suggestions.** All friendships have the potential to be wonderfully used for administering God's grace to one another, spurring one another on towards love and good deeds. However, this doesn't just happen automatically. Friendships can hinder us in our growth in godliness when we are bad examples for each other. We need to work hard at cultivating friendships that have a spiritual agenda, friendships which will be a blessing from God because Christ is at the centre. Such friendships will require a determination to be honest about ourselves and to seek the other's good by pointing them to the cross and all that we have in Christ, even when this means a gentle rebuke or warning.

# 8
## Ephesians 5; 1 Corinthians 6; 1 Thessalonians 4
# WOMEN AND THEIR BROTHERS

## THE BIG IDEA
Friendship between men and women in the church is to be characterised by love and purity.

## SUMMARY
In the face of overwhelming pressure from the world, God's people need to make every effort to avoid even a hint of sexual immorality, and to promote purity and brotherly love that will not wrong or take advantage of others. Free and full forgiveness is available to us as sexual sinners and we are to live holy lives in the light of that.

## OPTIONAL EXTRA
Discuss how sex is used to promote or sell things. You could provide a selection of magazines or show some TV adverts. Perhaps get your group to think of the most ludicrous or infamous advertising campaign that has used this kind of marketing. The purpose of this activity is to expose lies assumed by the advertising industry eg: buying a particular brand of chocolate/jeans/ perfume will make you sexually desirable; being a sexual temptress is a just a bit of fun that does nobody any harm.

## GUIDANCE FOR QUESTIONS
**1. How does the world around us encourage us to relate to men?** Although it is important and healthy to put time into friendships with both women and men, friendships with men can sometimes be confusing. This can be especially true in a world which is constantly telling us to view the opposite sex in terms of their potential

as partners or how attractive they are, rather than as human beings. The media, for example, gives very few good models of men and women relating as good friends, without flirting or having some kind of sexual agenda. Sex is splattered over everything and it is hard to remain unaffected in the way we view our sexuality and relationships with men. Being aware of this is vital to pursuing purity.

**2. What kinds of things should characterise the people of God?** Following God's example (v 1); love (v 2); sexual purity (v 3-4); goodness, righteousness and truth (v 8-9); aiming to please the Lord (v 10); exposing the deeds of darkness (v 11). **Why?** (1) Because God's wrath is going to come on those who are disobedient (v 6). (2) Because Christians have been rescued from the kingdom of darkness and brought into God's kingdom of light (v 8-14).

• **What kinds of things are "out of place" for the people of God?** Sexual immorality, impurity, greed (v 3); obscenity, foolish talk, coarse joking (v 4). **Why?** They are idolatry (v 5) and disobedience to God (v 6).

**3. APPLY: "But among you there must not be even a hint of sexual immorality" (Ephesians 5 v 3). List the implications for...** We must not miss how radical this teaching is in a society such as ours. "Not a hint of sexual immorality" has huge implications in so many areas of life. While we cannot leave the world, we can be more discerning about what we watch, read and learn from the world's attitudes towards sex, and be wise about how much we absorb without noticing. For each topic listed in this question, you could use a whiteboard/flip chart to compare things we will/won't do if we aim to please the Lord and show love to our Christian brothers versus if we aim only to please ourselves.

**4. What kinds of people were in the Corinthian church (verses 9-11)? What does this show about the gospel?** The Corinthian church included people who had previously lived wicked lives, as listed in verses 9-10. Various kinds of sexual immorality figure prominently, though not exclusively, in Paul's list of what it is to be wicked. This shows that the gospel is able to truly change people. This should be a great encouragement to those who struggle with guilt about their past way of life.

**5. How did they qualify for the kingdom of God (v 11)? How does this both encourage and humble us?** These wicked people were washed, sanctified (= made holy) and justified (= declared to be "not guilty" in God's sight). Notice that all these things were done for them and to them by the work of Christ and the Holy Spirit—they did not make themselves fit for the kingdom of God. This encourages us because no one is too sinful to be rescued and changed by the gospel. It humbles us because there is nothing that we can do to deserve a place in God's kingdom.

**6. Look at verses 11 and 19-20. How do they motivate us to live changed lives?** It is important to be sensitive in tackling this issue of sexual sin. It seems to have a long-lasting effect of guilt and emotional scarring unlike many other areas of sin. The wonder of the cross, as we see in the passage, is that

God is able to make people entirely justified (="just as if I'd never sinned"), however far off they may have been (v 11). Not only that, but the cross is also where we find our motivation to flee sin, in the knowledge that we were bought by God at such a great price (v 20).

**7. Think of as many reasons as you can for why Christians "go out" with someone. Which of these reasons do you think are wise, and which unwise?** Discussing the different reasons people can have for going out with someone else highlights the fact that many of our reasons are self-centred. They are fulfilling the emotional, physical or social needs of the moment. Clearly, it is not realistic to suggest that people should start out in a relationship with absolutely no thought for their own happiness. But there is a big difference between going out with someone for the pleasure, security and fun it brings now but with no thought of the future, and getting to know someone with a clear view to deciding whether or not to marry them. The former may not be considering the good of the other person first, and runs the risk of "leading them on", but the latter involves a commitment to making a decision which will either release the other person, or lead to marriage and devotion to the other's good for the rest of life together.

**8. From this passage, what should be the priorities for Christians who "go out"?** Pleasing God our Father is to be the ultimate priority (v 1), out of which come the concerns for sexual purity, self-control, distinctiveness and brotherly love. It may also help to brainstorm and then compare the world's priorities for a relationship.
**Note:** The danger and folly of going out with an unbeliever is worth mentioning

again, in discussing questions to be asked in deciding whether or not to go out with someone.

**9. Why does living in the world make it difficult to keep these priorities (eg: v 5)?**
We have to swim against a strong tide as we seek to please God and not ourselves in this area. The way in which Christians show love to each other when going out is totally opposite to how the world expects men and women in a relationship to "show love" (by having sex). Abstaining from sexual intimacy is commonly interpreted as a lack of love. However, notice how verses 4-6 expose the world's thinking for what it is—far from showing love, it reveals a lack of control over our own bodies and lusts, and takes advantage of the other person.

**10. How do you think that relating to one another as brother and sister transforms "going out" relationships? (v 6, 9, 10)?** It is worth having a look at 1 Timothy 5 v 1-2 with the group, as it is a great summary of relationships. It speaks of relationships among God's people as being like part of a family. Older men are like fathers; men of a similar age are like brothers to us. 1 Thessalonians 4 expands on this idea of being part of the same family—"brother" is mentioned five times in this chapter. We are not first and foremost "colleagues" or even friends, but family, not related by blood, but bound with even stronger ties—Christ's blood, making us one in Him. This should free us to have wholesome and warm relationships with Christian men. But note that for men relating to their sisters, Paul adds: "with absolute purity" (1 Timothy 5 v 2). He understands that as sexual beings, we are particularly vulnerable to temptation in our relationships with the opposite sex and need to be wise to this.

**11. APPLY: What do you think it looks like in practice to "avoid sexual immorality" in a relationship (v 3-4)?**
The common question in a relationship is often: how far can we go? The Bible answers "avoid" (v 3) and even "flee" (1 Corinthians 6 v 18) sexual immorality. We unthinkingly assume from the pattern of the world around us that physical intimacy is fine and appropriate in such a context. But there is very little, if any, biblical justification for this. It is always this worth remembering that the boyfriend now could be someone else's husband in the future, and to act accordingly.

**12. APPLY: You're advising a friend about being godly in a relationship with a man. How would you use 1 Thessalonians 4, and the other passages we have looked at, to advise them?** It is helpful to keep in mind that until a person is married, they are actually single and have an opportunity to serve God's kingdom with a freedom they won't have when they are married. This has implications for how time-consuming the relationship is. However, time will obviously be needed to develop the friendship in order to be in a position to make a decision about marriage. It is also worth thinking through how the principles of Ephesians 5 should be worked at in establishing habits of relating that will be a good foundation for marriage, albeit not to the same degree as in marriage. This will mean, for example, that the man is developing a pattern of initiative and responsibility in the relationship and the woman is enabling and encouraging him in this.

# 9

## Titus 2; Ephesians 6

# WOMEN AND THEIR CHILDREN

## THE BIG IDEA

Having children is a fundamental aspect of God-created womanhood, marred by the fall but redeemed in Christ, and a means by which women can be greatly used in raising the next generation to know Him.

## SUMMARY

Our God-created biological differences from men point to our helper role particularly in the area of bearing and raising children. This is hard because of the fall, but we are also given some beautiful examples in Scripture of what "redeemed" motherhood can look like when we are back in right relationship with God, and how the spiritual (as well as physical) nurture of children is a wonderful expression of our womanhood and a blessing to the next generation.

**Pastoral note:** It is worth saying that this topic, possibly more than any others covered in this study guide will, for some, be the most painful to look at. While it will be appropriate for women who currently have children, or women such as students who may well have children in the future, it may be difficult for more mixed groups where there are women who have not been able to have children. There will hopefully be good things for such women to learn in studying this topic in terms of finding other opportunities to be involved in the nurture of children, or in supporting those they know who are mothers, but it will need sensitivity to discern what will be most helpful and appropriate for the group. No doubt the pain of childlessness is also an

element of the curse of Genesis 3 v 16, which we all live in the light of. For those who are struggling with this pain, there is comfort in knowing the goodness and sovereignty of our loving God, and of using our God-given gifts of nurturing in other ways; for example, in the church family (with children, teenagers, or younger Christians), which can be a great blessing to God's people. This will hopefully be something to explore, particularly in question 11.

## OPTIONAL EXTRA

(1) Divide your group into sub-groups and ask them to list the joys and frustrations of motherhood (though bear in mind this would be inappropriate if members of your group are struggling with the reality of childlessness). You could divide the group between mothers and younger women who have not yet embarked on motherhood, and see how the two groups compare in their understanding of the realities of motherhood.

(2) Show a film excerpt which highlights some of the "not-a-bed-of-roses" realities of family life; eg: *Home Alone* (family supper the night before flying); *The Incredibles* (family dinner); *Cheaper by the Dozen* (virtually any scene in the film!). The aim is to highlight what a very mixed thing motherhood is—extreme joy and extreme frustration, which is true of all life post-fall.

## GUIDANCE FOR QUESTIONS

**1. List some of the positive and negative ways in which our culture**

views motherhood. Western culture has much to say about motherhood. On the one hand, it views it as a means of fulfilment, with the child as an idol to worship. On the other, it is seen as an inconvenient career break or even, according to some feminists, a form of domestic slavery.

Feminist thinking still pervades the value we place on the idea of motherhood being a woman's main profession. So the little girl who says: "When I grow up, I want to be a mummy" is considered rather quaint. A woman's right to have the most high-flying career she wants despite having children is generally assumed, dramatically impacting the way in which we raise our children. Therefore there has been a shift from home-based to institution-based care, and from seeing motherhood as a role distinct from fatherhood to a "co-parenting" approach. The work/home balance for mothers is a controversial area. In some cases, of course, the mother simply has to work outside the home, and sometimes it makes sense for a mother to work part time or a father to be involved in the daytime care of the children. The Bible, though, still pictures a unique role for mothers as those who have primary responsibility for day-to-day care of children, ensuring their needs are met and running the home they live in.

- **How do you think these views influence the decisions women make about having children?**

**2. How do Paul's words sound to our 21st century ears?** Paul's words sound completely out of date in our 21st-century western culture, but Paul does not suggest that what he says is purely cultural. These verses are supported by the rest of the Bible, from our creation design in Genesis 2 to examples such as the wife in Proverbs 31. There is no biblical prohibition on wives

being involved in work or other things outside the home; but the priority is to be the home.

**3. What kind of character is needed for fulfilling the role of wife, mother and homemaker so that all can see how attractive it is to live God's way?** Just ticking the boxes and doing our duty as wives, mothers and homemakers is not enough! The challenge of Titus 2 is to do this with love, self-control, purity, diligence, kindness and submission—all qualities that come from Christ and make our service beautiful.

## EXPLORE MORE

**Describe how this wife seeks to fulfil her role as a mother.** This woman clearly has a lot of different things going on in her busy life. On top of being a wife, mother and homemaker, she is also a businesswoman and compassionate to those in need. She even manages to look good (v 22b)! Her priorities, however are serving the needs of her family—her husband and her children, who call her "blessed" (v 28).

**What kinds of things might her children learn from her?** Seeing how to be, or to see the value of, a valuable and godly woman.

**What do you think it would be like to live in her home?** Her home is well-provided for (v 14-15, 21). There is much purposeful activity (eg: v 27). Relationships are respectful and healthy (v 11-12, 28), the home is hospitable and outward-looking (v 20, 23), and there is a sense of security (v 25). There is plenty to talk about and readily available advice (v 26). God is at the centre of the home (v 30).

**How do you think her relationship with the Lord underpins all she does?** Her "success" as a mother is not ultimately about her great multi-tasking skills, but about something available to every woman who knows God—she fears Him first and everything else flows from that.

**4. APPLY: How can understanding God's view of the role of motherhood help [women who describe themselves as "only a mum"]?** Having a right understanding of the importance of motherhood frees us from thinking, like the world, that changing nappies (or diapers), cooking meals, or playing in the garden are activities that are less significant than being a doctor or lawyer or other paid job (which is therefore seen as being "worthwhile").

**5. APPLY: Some mothers need to work full-time outside the home just to make ends meet; but where a mum has a choice, what principles and priorities should guide her decision?** Decisions about work need to be in the light of Christ's priorities and not compromise the role He has called us to as mothers, although what this looks like in practice will differ from woman to woman.

**6. APPLY: Where can we find opportunities to cultivate our God-given capacity for nurturing?**
• **Galatians 6 v 10:** Christians belong to a greater family than their biological relatives—the family of God, the church. Relationships within churches should bear a similarity to those within healthy biological families.
• **1 Timothy 5 v 10:** The widows mentioned here are past child-bearing age and yet still involved in both the upbringing of children, and nurturing the family of God, through hospitality and good deeds.
• **1 Thessalonians 2 v 6b-12:** Paul

describes his relationship with the Thessalonians who became Christians through his ministry in parenting terms, describing himself as both mother (v 7) and father (v 11) to them.

• **What attitudes can we learn from the wife of noble character?**

**7. What do these verses set out as the primary responsibility of parents?** The primary responsibility of a mother (under the leadership of her husband) is to raise her children in the Lord (v 2, 4). Although it is the primary responsibility of the father to ensure that the children are brought up in the "training and instruction of the Lord" (v 4), the mother is of course his vital helper in this (see Proverbs 6 v 20).
**Note:** In homes where there is no believing father, this task will fall to the mother alone (although she will certainly need the help and support of the church family). She can take encouragement from the example of Timothy's mother Eunice who, helped by her own mother, taught him the Scriptures from infancy, with no mention of a father being around.

• **How is this done?** Parents are to both "train" their children (give them practical teaching) and "instruct" them (give them knowledge).

• **What is the goal?** The goal is, first and foremost, children who will obey the Lord, which will be seen in their godly obedience to and honouring of their parents.

**8. Read the following Bible passages and note down anything they tell us about how or why parents are to teach their children about the Lord.**

| How we teach our children | Why we teach our children |
| --- | --- |
| **Deuteronomy 6 v 4-9:** Use as many opportunities as you can think of to "impress" your children with God's truth. | **Proverbs 6 v 20-22:** So that they will be kept safe from the dangers of sin. |
| **Deuteronomy 6 v 20-21:** Be ready to answer your children's questions about God and His ways. | **Proverbs 14 v 26:** So that they will find their security and stability in God. |
| **Psalm 145 v 4-7:** Celebrate, proclaim and even sing to your children about God's greatness and the things He has done for His people. | **2 Timothy 1 v 5; 3 v 15:** So that they will be saved through faith in Christ and live a life of faith in HIm. |

**9. How do all these verses show the parents' own relationship with God to be crucial in this task?** The great challenge for parents in teaching their children about the Lord is to make sure we are thinking about the Lord, so that we can talk naturally about Him. So, as Proverbs 14 v 26 encourages us, we need to be those who are first of all fearing the Lord ourselves, living consistent lives, and loving Him with heart, soul and strength—the pre-requisite Deuteronomy 6 v 5-9 gives us for teaching our children.

**10. APPLY: List some practical ideas for teaching children the Bible day to day. What kind of formal or informal, regular or unplanned opportunities can be taken?** We can't just assume this will happen automatically—parents are told to tell their children proactively about God and what He has done for us, making the most of every opportunity to share their faith with them. This can happen in all sorts of contexts, and in both formal and everyday conversations.

**11. APPLY: List some of the different ways in which Christian women might help in nurturing the children of others in Christ.** This challenge applies to the whole church family as we support one another in raising children to know the Lord. It's here that those who don't have children of their own can be of great help, whether as Sunday school/youth leaders, as godmothers, or simply as friends. Their lives and words can be a powerful witness, reinforcing what the children are learning at home, and providing more examples of what it looks like in different lives to love Jesus and follow Him.

# 10 Various; Luke 10 v 38-42

# WOMEN AND THEIR LORD

## THE BIG IDEA

We can and should grow in relationship with the most pro-woman man ever!

## SUMMARY

Jesus was radically different from His peers in the way He treated women with such honour, dignity and compassion. The women He met frequently responded to His tenderness and wisdom with devotion and faith. He wants us to grow in our faith and dependence on Him through making time to listen to Him, and thinking more about what He has done for us than what we might do for Him.

## OPTIONAL EXTRA

Get your group to make a list of five things in a day and three things in a week that they always do, no matter what. Compare lists and see which are the most popular answers. Discuss why you are so committed to doing those things. You could follow this up with making a list of three things in a day and one thing in a week that you would like to do, but rarely or never manage. (This activity serves as an introduction to question 1 and also relates to question 10.)

## GUIDANCE FOR QUESTIONS

**1. What are some of the things that threaten the priority of spending time with Jesus, in His word and prayer?**
• **What effect does it have on your life when time with God is squeezed out?** It is important to be aware that for some in the group the whole idea of "spending time with Jesus, in His word and prayer" may be quite new. This is something that

Christians do both privately and together as a church, though the New Testament speaks more often of corporate praying and Bible teaching than individual "quiet times".

**2. Look up the following passages and note down the kind of woman Jesus is with, how He relates to her and how she relates to Him.** See table over the page.

**3. Given that women did not have much social standing at this time, what strikes you about the women Jesus spoke to?** Jesus relates to all kinds of women, many of whom would have been completely rejected in their society for moral, social or ceremonial reasons. He treats each one with respect, gentleness and compassion, as He heals, teaches, forgives, comforts, restores and defends them. He even publicly commends some and holds them up as examples to be followed. Women respond to Him with awe and devotion as, with delight, they see in Him the most "pro-woman" man they have ever met.

**4. APPLY: Discuss what you've learned about the way Jesus relates to these women, and how they relate to Him. How does this encourage us as women who are known and loved by Jesus?** It is encouraging to know that, as with these women, there is nothing Jesus does not know about us, or cannot forgive about us. With Him we don't need to feel insecure or put on a "mask".

It is lovely the way Jesus also accepts the emotional responses of the women He

| Verse | What kind of woman | How Jesus relates to her | How she relates to Jesus |
|-------|--------------------|--------------------------|--------------------------|
| Luke 7 v 11-17 | A widow mourning her son's death (with no husband or son she had no means of support) | With compassion (raises son) | Not mentioned |
| Luke 7 v 36-50 | A sinful woman | He accepts her emotional way of honouring Him, and assures her that her sins are forgiven | She publicly and extravagantly shows her devotion to Him, in response to His forgiveness (v 47) |
| Luke 8 v 43-48 | Woman who's been bleeding for 12 years, so is religiously unclean and a social outcast (see Leviticus 15 v 25, 19) | He isn't angry that her touching Him made Him unclean—He heals her and calls her to Him to publicly commend her faith | Though trembling with fear, she obeys Jesus' call |
| John 4 v 1-26, 39 | Immoral woman (v 18) and, as a Samaritan, a woman hated by Jews | He reveals Himself to her as the living water that brings eternal life | She comes to understand Jesus' true identity and tells everyone she knows |

relates to. Several women cry on Him, some showing depths of emotion which many men would find awkward and embarrassing. Yet Jesus is never embarrassed or critical of women for responding like this. Tears are fully allowed with Him. We can be real and honest with the One who knows us best.

**5. Think about Martha: what had distracted her (v 40)? How did this colour what she thought about Mary and about Jesus?** It is interesting that Martha's preoccupation with what she was doing for Jesus distorted her view both of Him and of her sister. She accuses Mary of selfish neglect of her duty to help her sister, and even more shockingly, she accuses Jesus of not caring rightly for her (v 40). This can be so true of us, when service becomes a joyless, self-reliant burden causing us to feel cross and resentful towards Jesus and everyone else.

**6. How did Jesus respond (v 41)? What strikes you about His manner?** Jesus responds to Martha's accusing tones with extraordinary grace and patience. Instead of telling her off for failing to understand the right priorities and being anxious and resentful, He reasons with her. She had wrongly chosen to put more importance on what she was doing for Him rather than what He could do for her. She was distracted from Him by what she was doing for Him!

**7. What was Mary doing (v 39)? What was her attitude towards Jesus?** Mary, on the other hand, had "chosen what is better" (v 42). She had realised something that her sister had not, namely, that she needed Jesus. She knew she needed to listen to Him and learn from Him. Although many of us like to be activists who are always busy for Jesus, we need desperately to remember that nothing we do counts without such a relationship with Him as the foundation.

**8. What "better thing" had she chosen that Martha hadn't? Why would it "not be taken away from her" (v 42)?** The end of verse 42 also reminds us that investing time in our relationship with Jesus is never a waste of the time we could have spent "serving". It is always a good investment to listen to Him, and its value is for our eternal benefit.

**9. APPLY: What kinds of things distract us from Jesus and the "one thing needed"? How can we be like Martha in our attitude?** There are various reasons why we become distracted from the "one thing needed".

- Some in the group may be new to the idea of "spending time with Jesus, in His word and prayer". It is important to emphasise to such people that being a Christian is not about carrying out religious duties but about growing in a relationship with our Saviour and Lord.
- Most Christians will know how important it is to spend time with Jesus, but find that they are distracted by things which seem more urgent.
- For some people the difficulty is that they don't know how to go about praying or reading or listening to God's word.
- Some may have unrealistic expectations eg: devoting an hour a day to Bible-reading/listening and prayer when they have pre-school children and a non-Christian husband. They may have tried and failed previously and have given up because of discouragement.
- Some of us are like Martha, convincing ourselves that our busyness is all for the Lord anyway so lack of time spent with Him doesn't matter.

**Note:** This is also true of what can happen in church. Many Christians are so involved in serving (eg: teaching in Sunday school, running the creche) that they never have the opportunity to join in praise, prayer and learning from God's word with everyone else in a church meeting.

**10. APPLY: Think of all the priorities in your week (things which you always make sure happen). List four ways of also making sure that your time with Jesus happens.** No matter how full or busy life is, it's very rare for us to not make time to do the things we really and truly want to do. We need to recognise that we have more choice over how we spend our time than we often think we have. Once we have seen that spending time with Jesus is vital to our spiritual health, we can start to take responsibility, like Mary, for choosing "what is better" and making it our priority.

**11. APPLY: How can we make sure we do spend time with him (think practically)?** This is not meant to be another burden, just as spending time chatting to one's spouse or a Christian friend is not meant to be a burden, but an expression of love, commitment and the need to listen and talk to one another. Spending time "at Jesus' feet" may look different from person to person, and doesn't have to conform to a particular format, although there are many helpful aids and resources available. The basic ingredients are reading/listening to and thinking about part of the Bible, and speaking to God in prayer, with thankfulness, confession of sin and all sorts of requests. This can take all kinds of amounts of time and happen in all kinds of contexts. Commitment to church meetings—both on Sundays and mid-week—is also important, as well as seeking out more informal opportunities to do this together with others eg: a prayer partnership/triplet or resolving to spend 10 minutes praying with someone you meet regularly for coffee. Get your group to share ideas for the following (choose those most relevant to your group):

• how to organise a private time of prayer.
• how to read/listen to the Bible.
• when and where to pray and/or read/listen to the Bible together.
• how to benefit more from meeting as a church.
• how to encourage and make ourselves accountable to one another for spending time with the Lord.

**12. APPLY: How does the lasting value of this (v 42) encourage us to persevere in growing in our relationship with Jesus?** As we persevere in spending time with Jesus, we realise how much we need to do so, even though it often feels like (and in fact, is) a real battle! The benefits of spending time with Him are huge, enabling us to know how to please Him, to keep a right perspective (which Martha had all but lost) and motivation in serving Him, and to depend on His strength in everything. Like Mary, when we focus on all Jesus is, has done for us and promised to us, we will be more taken up with Him than with what we think we can do for Him. This is surely the best foundation for living for Him as women after His own heart.

**thegoodbook**
COMPANY

Opening up the Bible

| NORTH AMERICA |  thegoodbook.com |  866 244 2165 |
| UK & EUROPE | thegoodbook.co.uk | 0333 123 0880 |
| AUSTRALIA | thegoodbook.com.au | (02) 6100 4211 |
| NEW ZEALAND | thegoodbook.co.nz | (+64) 3 343 2463 |

 **WWW.CHRISTIANITYEXPLORED.ORG**
Our partner site is a great place for those exploring the Christian faith, with a clear explanation of the good news, powerful testimonies and answers to difficult questions.